TONY GROGAN'S
VANISHING CAPE TOWN

Text: BRIAN BARROW

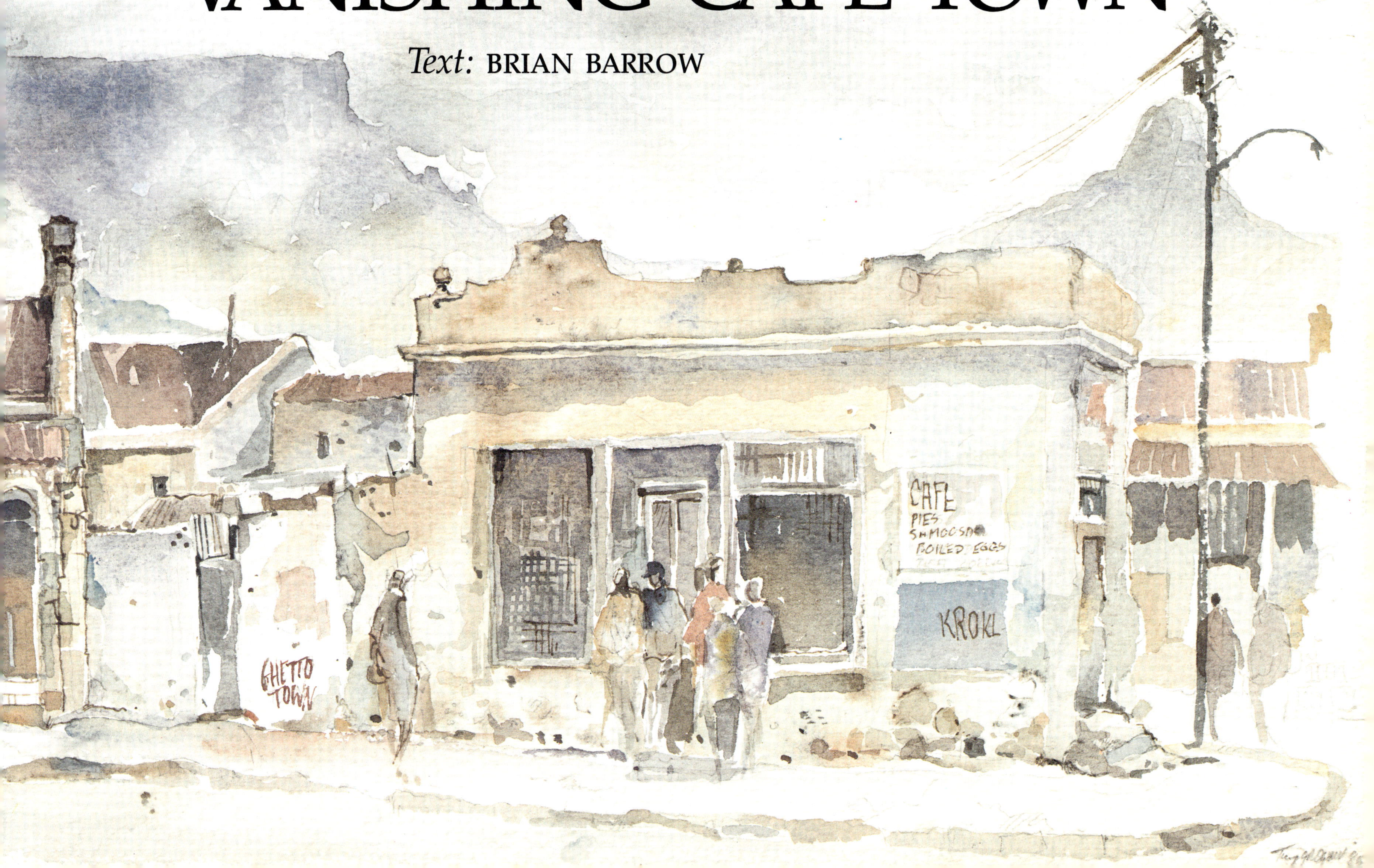

Also by Tony Grogan

Vanishing Villages
Settler Country
South African Sketchbook

Palm Tree Mosque
Long St.

ISBN 1 86806 007 1

First edition 1976
Second impression 1979

Second edition 1985
Second impression 1988

Published by Don Nelson
P O Box 859, Cape Town 8000

Copyright: Tony Grogan and Brian Barrow

Printed and bound by Galvin & Sales, Cape Town

To Jen

Introduction

MANY people feel that a lot of modern art has run into a cul-de-sac of frustration and repetition. Too many artists have tried to jump onto every trendy bandwagon rather than rely on their own instincts and talents. They have considered it more important to be "with it" than to be themselves.

Cape Town can be glad that this never happened to Tony Grogan, not that there was ever any chance of it happening, for Grogan, a modest and unpretentious man, could never be anything but himself.

As an artist more technically equipped than most, he works from his own individual vision and the result is honest and altogether charming. The subjects that have attracted him are the ordinary people of this city who have always given it so much life, and many of the delightful old buildings and street scenes that are still the joy of Long Street, Loop Street, Bree Street and others, as well as the Malay Quarter, Woodstock and what is left of District Six. Most of his pictures have been painted or drawn since his arrival in Cape Town early in 1974, so he is not only the most recent painter of South Africa's most painted city, but probably one of the last who will have anything left to paint before the developers move in.

Many of his works have already found their way into some of our best private collections. His colours are subdued, but serve his purpose with economy and good taste. He has captured the atmosphere and mood of his subjects with joy and spontaneity.

No words can ever do full justice to Tony Grogan's work, so in collaborating on this book, no direct reference has been made to any of his paintings or drawings. We decided that it would be far better if each of us tried to portray the concept of Vanishing Cape Town in his own way, in the hope that words and pictures would complement each other.

There was one aspect of Cape Town, however, for which we felt the same concern, and that was what appears to be the deteriorating quality of its social environment.

Brian Barrow

Flower Sellers

Wash day - Malay Quarter.

Tony GROGAN '76.

Wynberg, Cape.

The Fireman's Arms

Klaus Lucas in contemplative mood

Mrs Gladyshe

Corner of Long & Church St.

Long Street.

Fish Market – District Six

Cut Lovers with novel headgear

lunch time interlude - District Six

Loop Street.

Fruit Vendors, Claremont.

"Apples, fife fora bwab".

Bree St, Crofts antique shop.   Tony Grogan '76

The Café Royal.

Man with a trolley.

District Six.   Tony Grogan '76.

Mr & Mrs Kashew – Oxsole Shoe Repairs

Washerwoman - Nordsvaag washhouse *Tony Grogan*

Mr. Ibrahim Mustapha - Riley Taylor. *Tony Grogan '76.*

Malay Quarter, Cape.   Tony Grogan 1985

Dalmar Estate. Tony Grogan.

Dockside girls

Catching Harders

Five cent ferry

Feeding terns

Plein St., Cape Town.

Tony Grogan 1976

Florence Frazer

Maggie Plaatjies

Long Street, Cape Town

Tony Grogan '86

Strand Street, Cape Town.

Service dining room - kitchen.

Tony Grogan '16

Fish Market - District Six.

Tony Grogan '76.

"District 6, Cape.

Salt River, Cape   Tony Grogan '76

Good Hope Cash Store – Salt River.

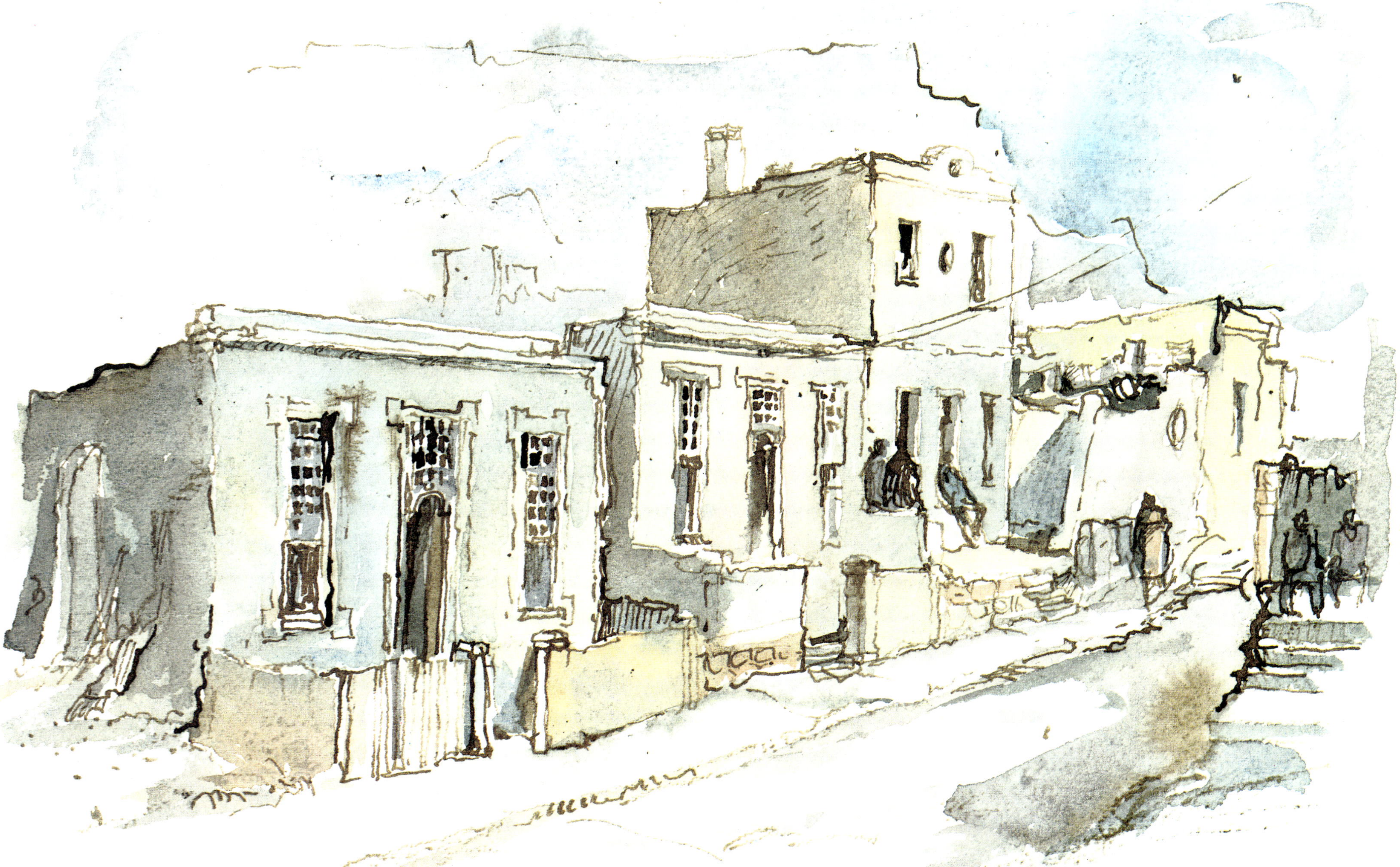

Malay Quarter.

Tony Grogan

'Argy-bate!'

Newsstand - Main Station

Greenmarket Square.

Malay Quarter — Tony Grogan '76

Malay Quarter, Cape   Tony Grogan '76

Boesman Parade takes a nap.

"Emma-ka-lemma"

The 'Odds and Sods' stall - Grand Parade.

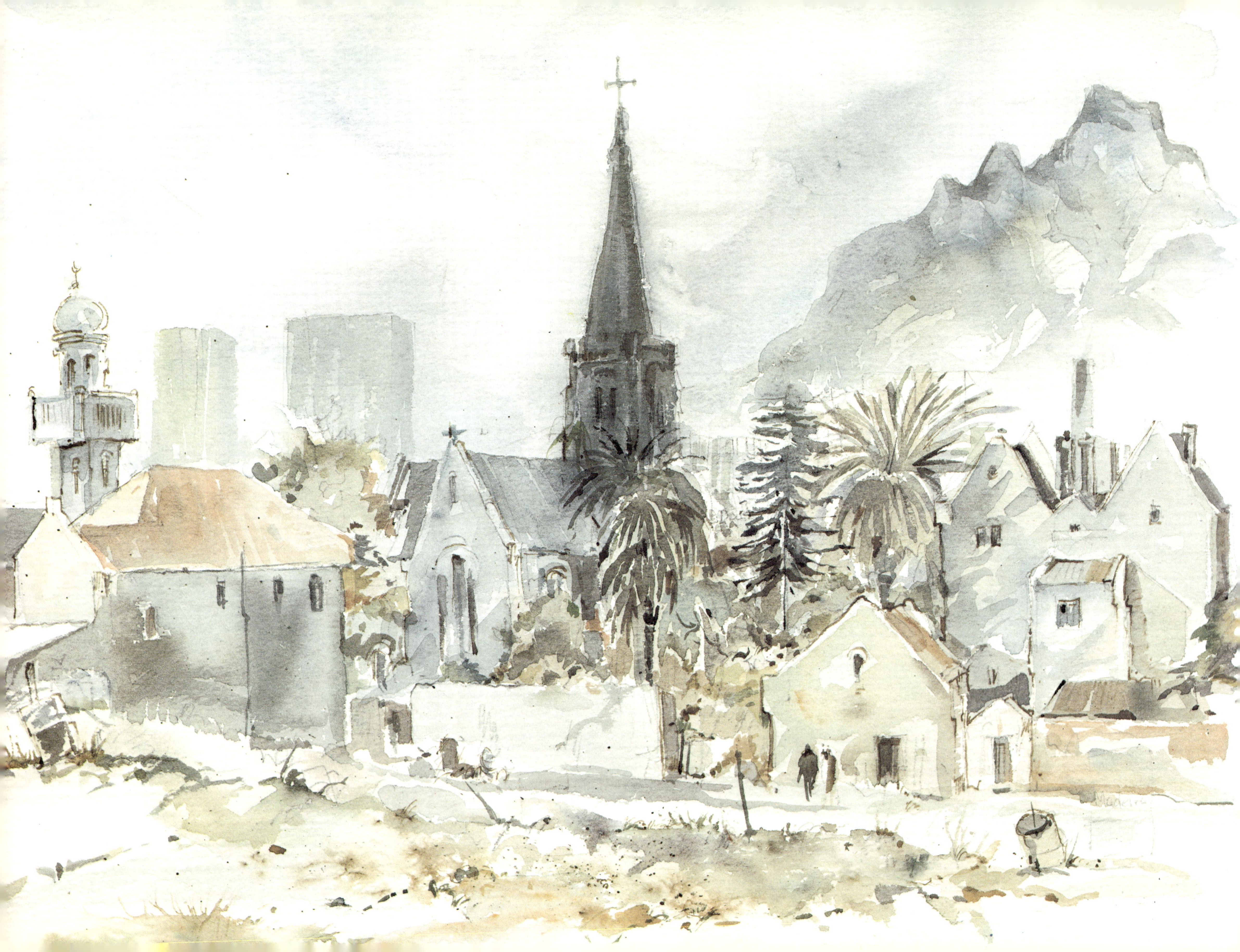

District 6 - Last days.

"The Godfather of
Woodstock, 'Porkchops'."

"My Sweet Mary & Funny Man".

Lower Main Rd, Woodstock

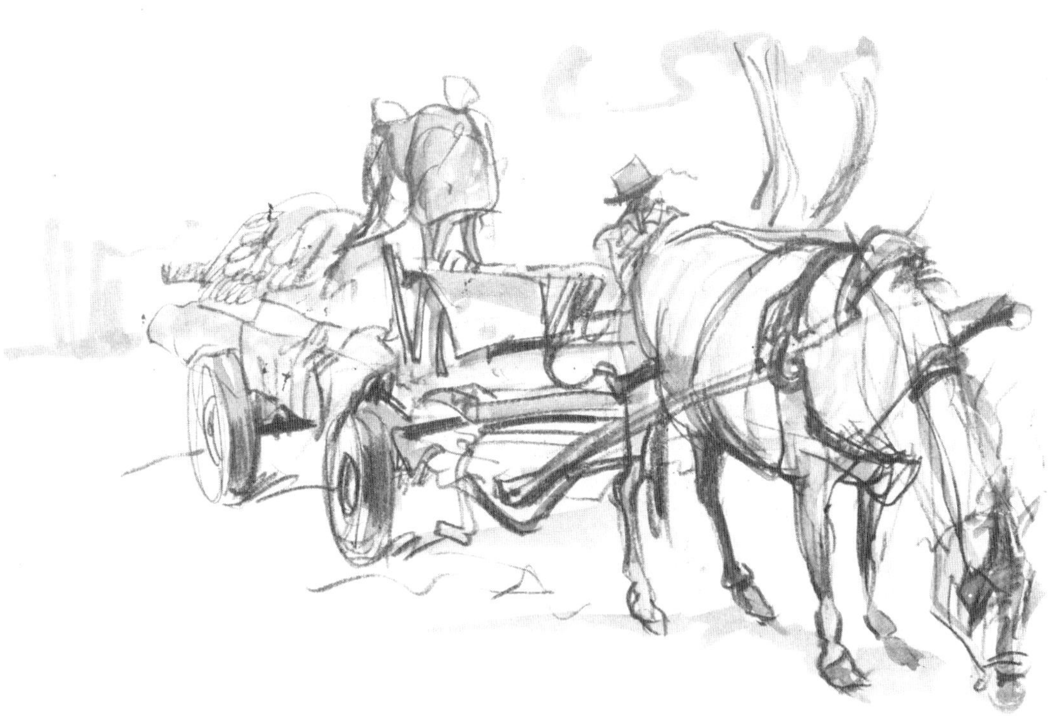

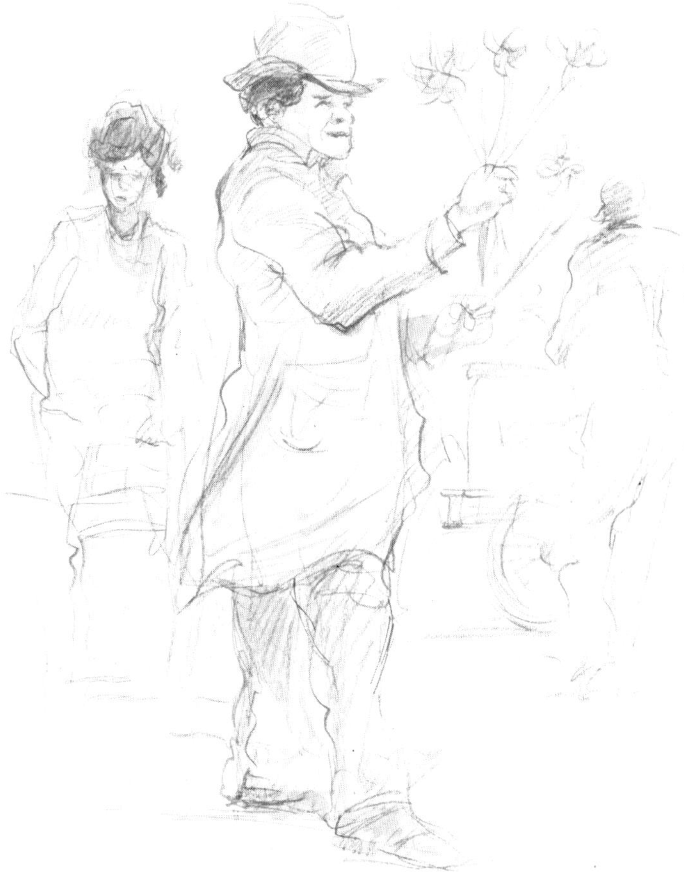

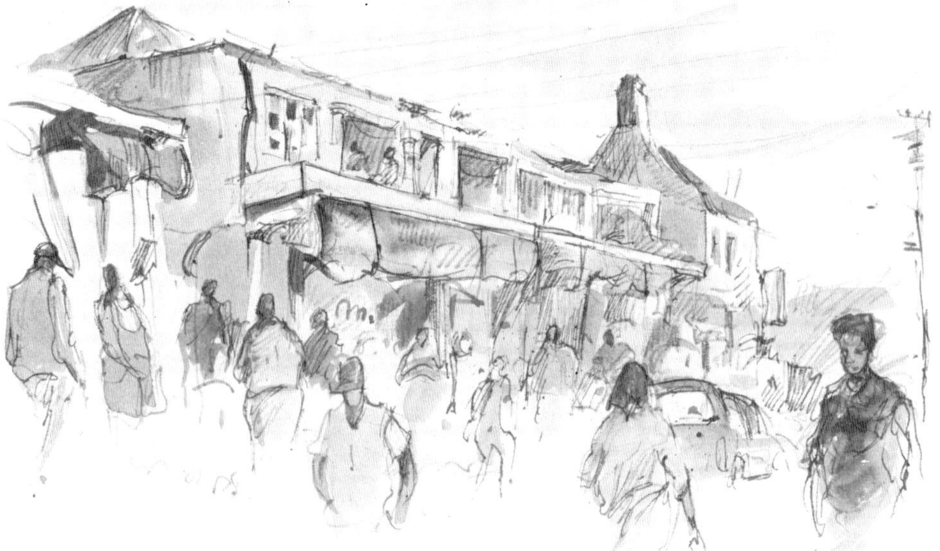

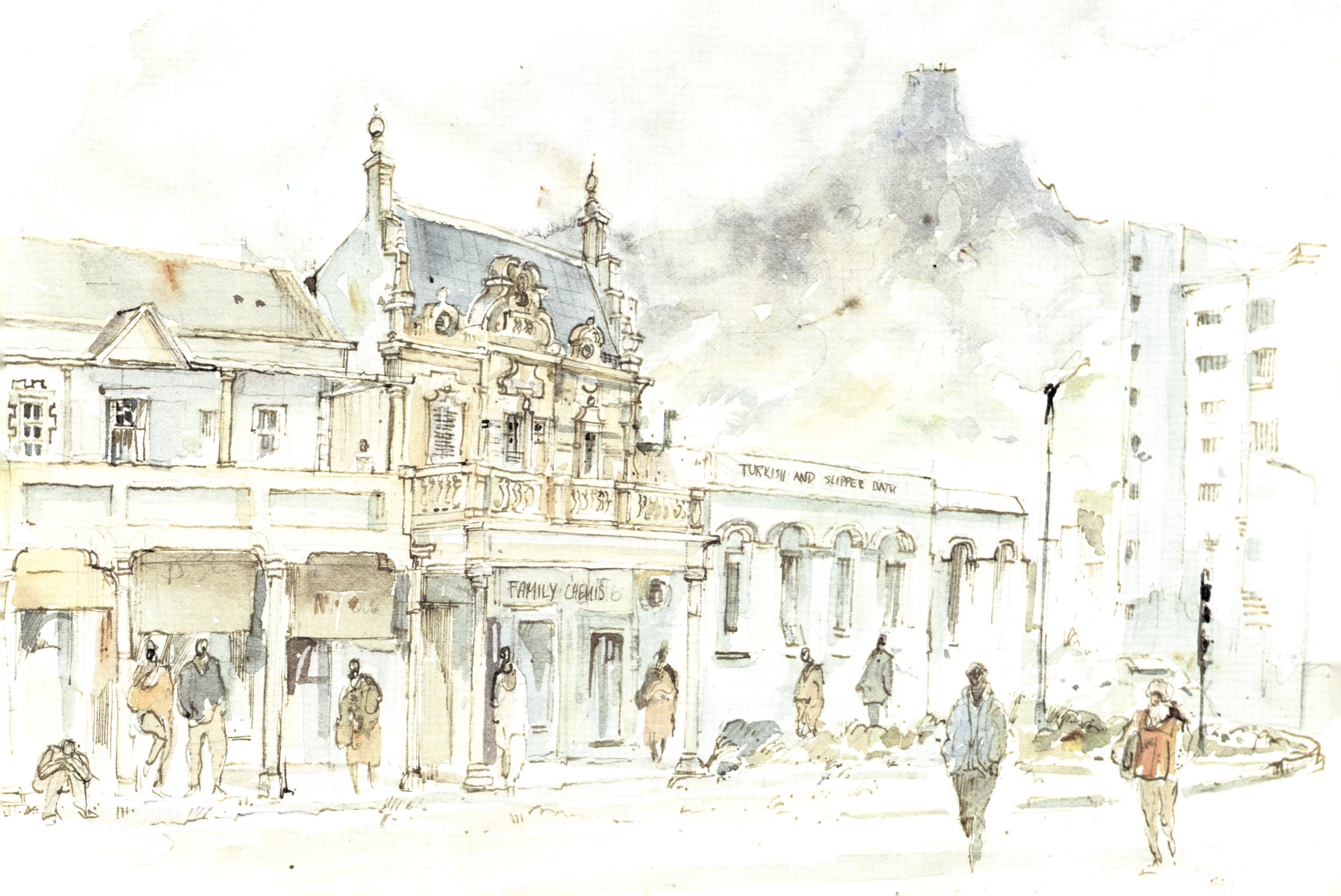
TURKISH AND SLIPPER BATH
FAMILY CHEMIS

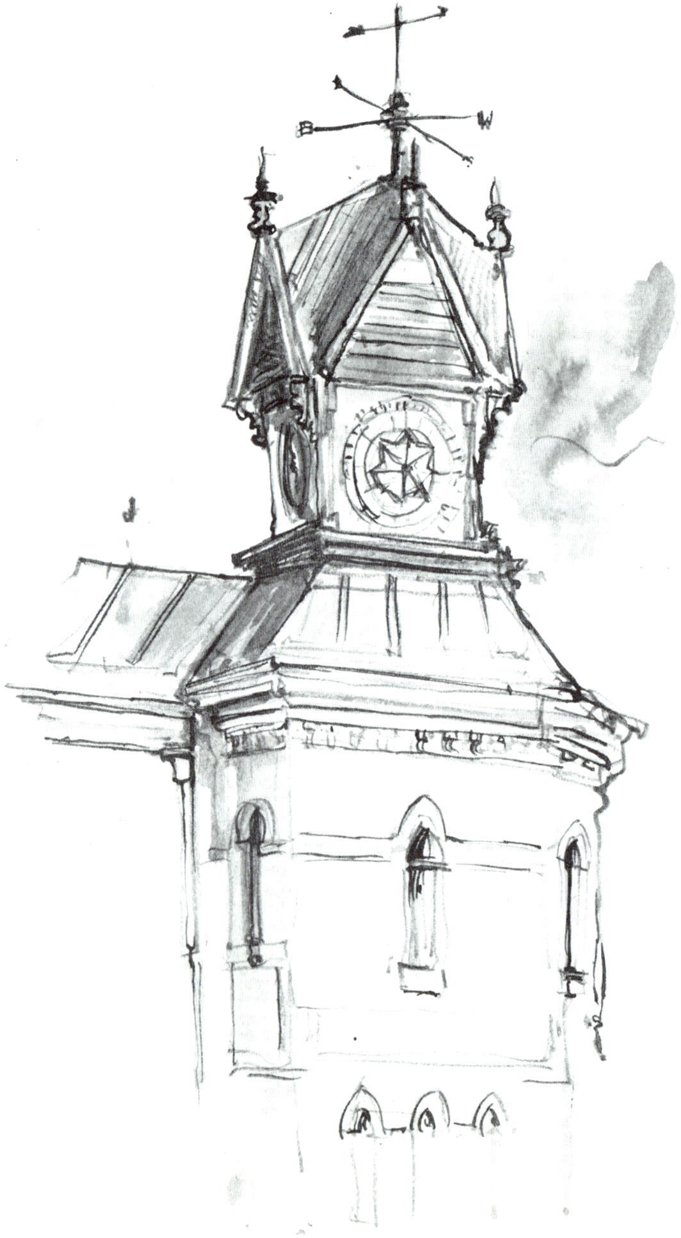

The Old Clock Tower

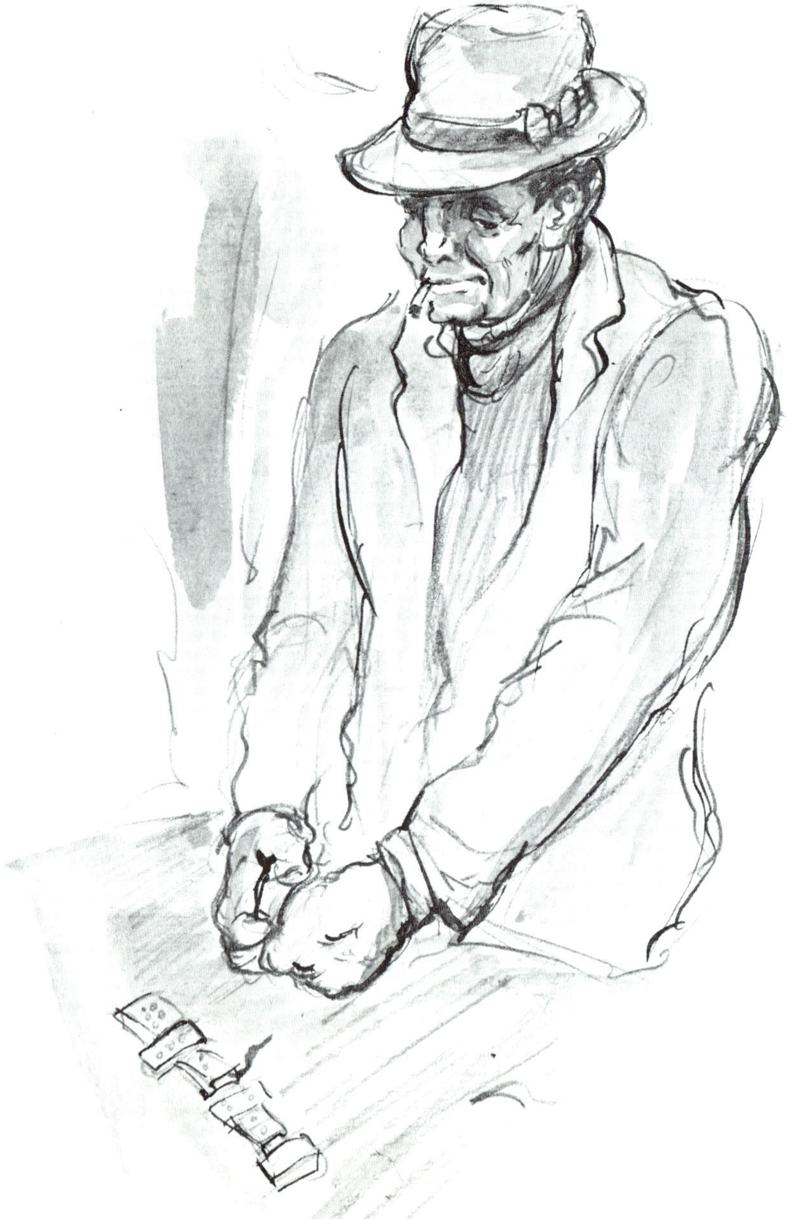

Playing dominoes.

Service Lane - Salt River

Tony Grogan '76

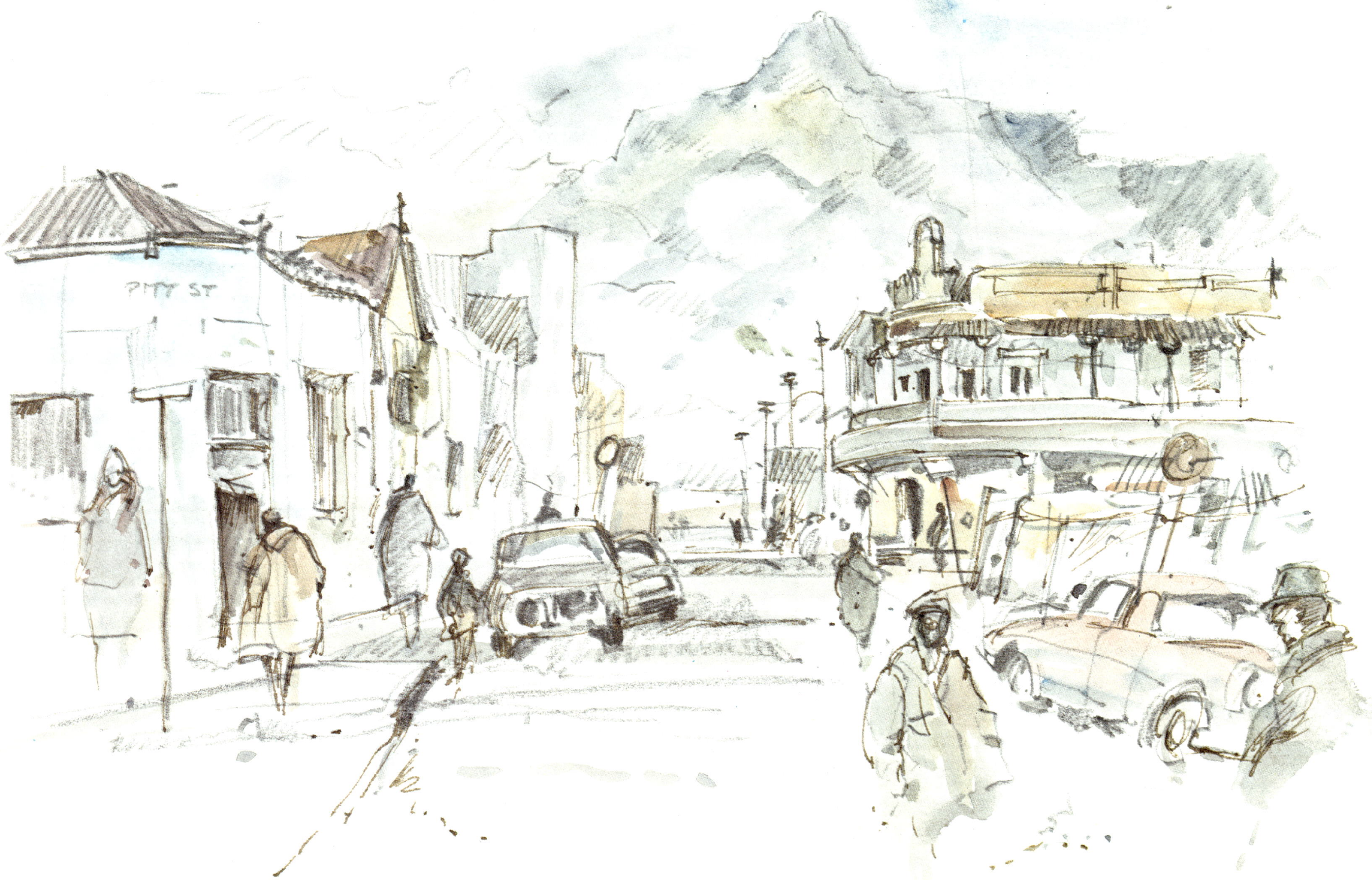
PITT ST

Nostalgia

THERE has been an intense curiosity in recent years about Cape Town as it was during the eighteenth and nineteenth centuries, even about Cape Town at the turn of the century and before the last World War. For some the interest has been purely historical, for others it has been aesthetic and for many it has been woven into an acute awareness of a cultural heritage.

There is something reassuring about having a cultural heritage of our very own, one that grew out of the soil of the White man's Africa, one that could be so easily discovered among all the gables and the grapes of the Western Cape. This is where it all began for us in Southern Africa, and it is therefore necessary and desirable for the spiritual enrichment of present and future generations that the validity of it all should be affirmed and reaffirmed.

And there is no harm in that. In fact, it is doing all of us a great deal of good. It is an attractive parcel from our past wrapped around with charm and beauty in a certain unique style. There is romance in it too, and above all, that vital link with the past.

In many ways the curiosity has become a mania bordering on a kind of sentimental nostalgia that will see a lost paradise in an old soda-water bottle or an act of sacrilege in the demolition of a dilapidated dwelling, as if the final act of destruction is more reprehensible than the long years of neglect. But the curiosity remains in all its guises among growing numbers of people and for all the idiosyncrasies that often go with it, it is a wholly genuine and worthwhile sentiment.

It has produced things we can be thankful for. Old diaries, letters and journals have been published in book form and found many proud buyers. Any book about the life in the Cape, or anywhere else in South Africa, before 1900 is a valuable acquisition. Old tools, eating utensils, kitchenware or china is dearly sought after. Cape silver, glassware, brass as well as old drawings, paintings, prints or photographs have quite rightly become things of value, both sentimental and actual. Practically any household object more than seventy years old can qualify as Africana and a whole new race of collectors has appeared on the scene.

Some of them, rather selfishly and unscrupulousy, have scoured the countryside to buy up fine old pieces of furniture for a song from poor or ignorant people who haven't realized the value of what they've sold. Faked Cape-Dutch furniture has found its way onto the floors of certain antique dealers and sold as the genuine thing. As for the restoration of old buildings, and even buildings that are not so old, this has almost become a redemptive need. Fortunately it has also become a most respectable and worthwhile cause on which the cultured rich can spend their money.

Has there ever been such a yearning and search for the past? Often when it cannot be found, it is recreated. It must be symptomatic of some deep need. It is as if South Africans, having settled into a very pleasant and easy way of life, are turning towards their past to justify it. There is always so much reassurance in the past as the foundation stone of the present and there is the constant wish to identify with it. But why has the need become so intense and widespread?

I can but venture an explanation which can only be a small part of the whole explanation. I think people, especially in Cape Town, suddenly began to feel that a huge gulf was separating them irrevocably from the past.

The feeling probably began after World War II and it intensified with the new values and life-styles that came in the following decades. There was a sudden feeling of estrangement from an accustomed way of life and at the same time the imposition of something new and strange. Far more swiftly than they could ever realize, the whole atmosphere and environment of this loved, leisurely, easy-going city of grace and dignity was changing and would never be the same again.

A building of historical and sentimental content would be reduced to an open space by the demolishers before anyone could do anything about it. And the open space they saw was like a wound. It hurt. The new building rising in its place would never be anything but a scar.

People began to realize that something they had grown attached to was being removed for good. The little that remained was precious. But too much was lost, far too much, before they realized how precious it was.

Of course, they should have realized what was happening, but they didn't, or pretended not to. How could they have known, anyway? The reshaping of a city is something beyond the average man's comprehension and immediate interest. Often he doesn't know it is happening till the pub he has visited for years isn't there any more. He is mostly not aware of the economic considerations that hasten change. Owners want to sell at a profit, the developers who move in want their returns and the local authority wants its revenue. Also, change is a subtle, sneaky, if not methodical process which few people recognize until it begins to pronounce itself in the harsh language of reinforced concrete, rising higher and wider like the faceless walls of a prison. Their relationship with their city environment is never quite the same again.

I have experienced this myself and the reaction I have felt has been one of sadness and nostalgia, a pointless reaction perhaps, but one which forces you to look back and try and understand. The whole history of Cape Town has been one of constant change and adaption. But the difference has been that up to now change had always been a smooth and logical process and growth has been so slow that people have always been able to keep pace with it emotionally.

Apart from a certain amount of ornamentation, building methods and styles didn't change much in the old days. At any rate, no new building was so jarringly different that it threatened the ordinary man's deeply rooted idea of what a building should look like; it always fitted into the popular concept of what was artistic and tasteful.

In those days architecture was still very much an art, although a rather stagnant one, and not a massive feat of engineering. Its most important function was to serve people, to provide them with shelter from the elements for the purpose of living, working, worship and recreation.

It was not till the end of the 1890s that the new ferro-concrete concept of architecture began to change the horizontal lines of cities into vertical ones. Even then it took many years before the new epoch-making techniques were applied in Cape Town and not till after the last war were they given full reign, thrusting concrete squares and rectangles into the sky, dwarfing and isolating the older buildings, making people insignificant and even pretending to emulate the majesty of Table Mountain.

But for the moment we are concerned with the past and what it was like. For the sake of those who wish to do so, let us indulge briefly in one of those pleasant reveries of a Cape Town that has all but vanished before we get too involved with the Cape Town that is vanishing before our very eyes.

Writers, artists and travellers have left us rich impressions of Cape Town as it was in the late eighteenth and early nineteenth centuries, but it is still tempting to bend back the imagination and dwell on the mood, pace and atmosphere of those days. It helps if one studies the works of the many artists who recorded what they saw. One can also play a fascinating game, looking at old plans of the town and trying to see how places like the Castle, the Old Town House, Koopmans de Wet House and the Lutheran Church group fitted into the general picture, say, at the beginning of the nineteenth century which is a good starting point.

In the year 1800, most of the town was still confined to its eastern and western limits, Buitenkant Street and the Buitengracht. Most of the landmarks we know today were there: the old company gardens, the Castle with its jetty, the Grand Parade, Greenmarket Square, known then as Market Square (and what a lively market it was), Riebeeck Square, known then as Hottentot Square where all the farmers outspanned their wagons, and Church Square. The Parade extended west as far as the Heerengracht, now Adderley Street and it was bordered by trees.

It appeared to be an extremely neat and orderly town with the streets crossing one another at right angles as they do now. Long, Loop and Bree streets ran right down to the Bay which curved into the town with the shore not more than a couple of hundred metres from Strand Street and the Parade. Wale Street and Waterkant Street were both there, so was Keerom Street and Queen Victoria Street, then called Tuin Street as it ran parallel to the Company Gardens. Roeland Street was there too and so was Stal Plein and the beginnings of Government House.

A later map drawn roundabout 1825, shows some very interesting places like the Town Shambles, between the Parade and the sea which must have been the abattoirs and meat market because a Shambles was, according to an old dictionary "any place of slaughter and carnage".

The maps tell us that it was a gay and lively town. There was the theatre in Riebeeck Square (St Stephen's Church), there were several taverns including the George's Hotel and the Beaufort Arms Hotel, a menagerie where wild animals were kept for exhibition, a town granary and storehouse, a customs house down at the bay, the Commercial Exchange, a prison, a post office, three hospitals including one for the military and one for merchant seamen and no fewer than seven churches or chapels. The Old Town House was then the Burgher Senate House. The place never changed much for the next fifty years.

The more intimate glimpses come to us from the artists of those times who captured its human warmth and its atmosphere. There is a beautiful picture by W. Langschmidt showing us the top of St George's Street round about 1845 with the old St George's Cathedral facing us and the dark buttress of Table Mountain in the background, jutting into a pink sky.

The cathedral is a fine sight with its beige coloured walls, its six giant columns supporting the frieze and handsome pointed pediment, and the slender tower with columns diminishing in size, rising against the sky. With what authority it affirmed the Christian faith and dominated the street. A dark shadow falls diagonally across its facade, giving a touch of drama. It blends with the three-storeyed houses on the left of the street, one of them a private home with an arched fanlight above the doorway and a raised front stoep. The walls of the house are bright pink. A gentleman in a top hat and frock coat sits on the stoep. On the opposite side of the street are two brick-red buildings.

In the street itself are a number of people: men in top hats, a soldier, women with bonnets, wide skirts and parasols, a group of Coloured women wearing white bodices, puffed sleeves and long skirts of blue, pink and green. There's a dog. Two men are in conversation. A Malay man is carrying baskets of vegetables. A building on the extreme left could be a tavern. Its doors are open and people are wandering in and out. It is a heart-warming picture.

The scene was very much the same when Arthur Elliott took a photograph of the cathedral in the 1890s. For years the Cathedral was one of Cape Town's finest landmarks. What a pity it isn't still there. It was demolished after the last war because they said it was crumbling and unsafe. It was neither. The demolishers found it an extremely tough building to break down. It resisted their onslaughts to the very last. When finally they flattened it, St George's Street was never the same again. The unremarkable edifice of stone we have in its place is a poor successor even if it was designed by Sir Herbert Baker.

What glorious spaciousness Cape Town had in those days; how clean the air and the flanks of Table Mountain, Lion's Head and Devil's Peak. There were no buildings prominent enough to draw the eye away from the mountain's dramatic splendour. There were no plantations of grizzly pines on its slopes. It appeared to be so much higher. From the town itself it must have seemed overpowering and colossal. From the way some of the early artists depicted it, you'd think that the sight of it filled them with terror. In one of his pictures, William Hodges RA seemed to see it as one of the ramparts of Hell. He distorted it into something awesome and satanic. Perhaps it was his mood at the time for some of his other pictures give us a far more benign mountain.

A picture by William John Huggins on the other hand, painted about 1815, of East Indiamen entering Table Bay, shows quite a different view of the mountain amphitheatre sweeping down to the bay. Devil's Peak, Table Mountain, Lion's Head and Signal Hill look as harmless as loaves of bread. One wonders why the mountain did not strike the artist more forcibly. In a picture of a merchantman arriving in Table Bay roundabout 1818, Thomas Whitcombe distorts the mountain groups into a most unimpressive arrangement of shapes too narrow to be real.

There's another painting by Langschmidt of a section of Long Street with the very clean and accurate representation of Devil's Peak in the background. In the foreground are flat-topped, single-storeyed dwellings with whitewashed walls and green doors and shutters. Each house is entered by a narrow footbridge leading from the street to the stoep and beneath the bridges flows a stream of water. There is a Malay man with baskets carried by means of a pole across his shoulders. The south-easter cloud is gathering round Devil's Peak. It is late afternoon and the walls of the buildings are aglow with a saffron light.

There are some water-colours by Henry Clifford de Meillou, dating from about 1825 which still convey to us the restful atmosphere of the town, one of the best being of Greig's Bookshop from the Parade with the Lutheran Church tower in the background. And we are indebted to Samuel Daniell for his superb lithograph of the theatre in Hottentot (now Riebeeck) Square. The mountain forms a pale blue backdrop.

There is an ox-wagon in the foreground and the square itself is filled with a rich light which falls on the buttressed west wall of the theatre. For me this picture describes the mood and pace of those times in a very moving and intense way.

Most of these pictures, by the way, can be seen in the Fehr Collection which is housed in the Castle and in Rust-en-Vreugde in Buitenkant Street. Another one I can look at again and again is a water-colour by Samuel Davis of the Fiscal's home at the corner of Strand Street and Burg Street.

In the foreground, an ox-wagon is rounding the corner from lower Strand Street into Burg Street and there is a coach drawn by four horses. The Fiscal's house looks typically Cape-Dutch. It is double-storeyed with a basement on Strand Street. It is painted in a lime-coloured wash with green doors, shutters and window frames. It has an ornate parapet with a balustrade and Grecian urns on top. There's a charming hint of pomposity which well becomes a fiscal.

There are some fine panoramic views of the town. One was drawn by Captain Walter Stanhope Sherwell from the roof of the Lutheran Church in Strand Street. In it we see a town of unique beauty and character. Could there have been any other place in the world like it? I don't think so.

The sweep of the bay, the bold mountain trinity, and joining them a town, whitewashed and brilliant in the sun, of broad busy streets and classical proportions. The streets are alive: wagons, horse-drawn coaches, men on horseback, oxen drawing two-wheeled carts, pedestrians and Malays in conical hats carrying baskets of produce. The buildings with flat roofs are mostly three-storeyed and of fairly uniform design and along many streets there are rows of trees.

There are two exciting street scenes: one offers a view down Strand Street towards the Parade, the other shows Bree Street and Buitengraght converging towards Lion's Head. In the middle distance we can see the towers of St George's Cathedral and the Groote Kerk, I think, and also the outline of St Mary's although one cannot be quite sure.

To me this picture represents Cape Town as a place of tranquil loveliness with noble proportions. Its essentially eighteenth century character was still there, the new building styles introduced with British rule had not yet made their full impact. If it had been possible to retain its character as it was then (and I realize that it was, in fact, impossible) it would today be one of the most enchanting cities in the world. But it was not possible. It had no hope of passing down to future generations its indigenous eighteenth century flavour and atmosphere. Even then it was expanding. The second British occupation brought with it a wave of expansion and the old Dutch vernacular style of building gave way to prevailing English fashions. Georgian houses appeared with tall windows and decorative fanlights. Pitched roofs returned and later houses were surrounded by broad verandahs with wrought-iron railings, gates and balconies.

By the middle of the nineteenth century Cape Town was bursting into a rash of chaotic building styles. Dwellings became more English in character and public building was influenced by all kinds of architectural revivals: neo-Grecian, Roman and Gothic which became increasingly popular. The Georgian era which somehow blended with eighteenth century Cape Town was ending and Victorian ideas were finding favour with their love of excessive ornamentation.

There was the most incredible diversity of styles, including the revival of the Egyptian in one or two cases and most of them were foreign importations from Britain. The place was infested with scrolls, drapery, Grecian urns, baroque curves, Gothic arches and mass-produced decorations: imitations of Italian renaissance and classic patterns from Rome, Venice and Florence. The embellishment eventually became embarrassing.

And yet, strangely enough, the outcome was not as depressing as it might sound. By the end of the nineteenth century Cape Town, after all the architectural onslaughts that had been made upon it, still retained its intimacy and charm and surprisingly it still had tremendous character even if it had lost its original purity.

It is surprising that the city survived the sheer weight of all the ornamentation that covered just about every public and commercial building: the pilasters, the pedestals, the variety of pediments, the arches and columns with their composite capitals, the balconies supporting tons of decorative iron work, the parapets and the balustrades, the ornamental consoles and heavy cornices, the mouldings, dentils, foliations and frills. There was almost an excrescence of embellishment.

With the new wave of prosperity after the Anglo-Boer War, there was another rash of building between 1900 and 1910 and the early twentieth century saw the era of "art nouveau" in South Africa with even more decoration imported from Britain and Europe.

There had to be a reaction and it came, of course, in the 1930s with the new architecture of efficiency and economy of style – the beginning of the purely functional age.

How could old, charming eighteenth century Cape Town have possibly survived the monumental accretions of style that were superimposed on it and which finally smothered and destroyed it. It seems to me that the Cape Town of our romantic illusions began to die about the mid-nineteenth century and that there was very little left of it by the end of that century.

What amazes me is that there are still so many of us who still talk about preserving old Cape Town. Our capacity for self-delusion knows no bounds, even in the face of concrete facts. There are scores of us who think that old Cape Town still exists. The truth is that it doesn't. It has gone forever.

Many of the old eighteenth century dwellings disappeared quite naturally in the course of time, long before most people saw any beauty or value in them. After all, to the people who lived in them they were not future national monuments, they were homes. And they had less chance of withstanding the severity of the Cape winters than modern homes. Their upkeep must have been difficult and expensive. They were changed, often they were enlarged and sometimes they were knocked down or sold and replaced by better-built homes. Even in recent times, no-one has had the power to prevent their destruction.

A fair number of Cape Dutch buildings were left in Cape Town at the beginning of this century, but by 1960 there were not more than a couple of dozen. Three bodies have done excellent work trying to preserve them: the Historical Monuments' Commission, the South African National Society and the Simon van der Stel Foundation, but none of them has had the power to save houses from destruction. With the exception of museums, historical monuments like Koopmans de Wet House and old houses still standing in the suburbs, Cape Town has lost nearly all the buildings that gave it its dinstinctive architectural character.

In the central city there are only ten eighteenth century buildings left and most of them are vulnerable because they do not form complexes; they stand in total isolation and there is little hope that they will survive. Most of them are so dwarfed by modern buildings all around them that they are divorced from their historical context and are therefore declining cultural assets. They are sad, lonely buildings which appear to be losing their usefulness and all of them stand on sites that cannot escape the greedy eyes of the developers. It seems, in fact, that the developers can do whatever they like if people will let them. There's not so much as an old Dutch gable left to restrain them.

Anyone who still thinks that there is anything left of eighteenth and early nineteenth century Cape Town, is living in a cultural afterglow that is purely imaginary.

Cape Town has changed because the world has changed and South Africa has changed. It is still changing and it is futile trying to put back the clock. We have to accept the modern world and be part of the society which the modern world is shaping to its own needs and uses. We might lose much in the process, but we might gain something too. But what we must not accept is the dehumanization that appears to be creeping into our big cities with every new concrete monolith.

Architectural change has been inevitable and unavoidable. People always understood and accepted that. It has always been obligatory to genuflect before the God of Progress. In fact, people got used to it years ago when the process of destruction was slower and more dignified. In those days demolition was a polite business. Old buildings died discreetly and they usually went one at a time, so the shock was not really unbearable. It often took weeks to level them. Everyone had time to adjust. The new buildings that replaced them might have been bigger, but they were not gigantic monuments to one architect's genius, nor did they have a desolating effect on the whole environment.

But since about 1960, urban development has become quite a different kind of operation and its reverberations have been heard and felt by nearly everyone. Destruction, or to put it more gently, demolition has become an industry in itself. Big firms began to specialize in the job. Huge new machines designed for the purpose arrived at certain places and their job was not to destroy single buildings, but to sweep away entire blocks and often whole communities, regardless of the social warmth and cohesion they gave to a city. This kind of destruction was too much. It was traumatic in a way, it wasn't what people had come to accept as change. It was more like revolution. So were the new great structures of concrete and glass that rose from the dust – monuments of the architectural revolution that is changing every large city in the world.

In the last fifteen years, Cape Town has been transformed by these islands in the sky. They are not only changing the physical profile of the city, but changing its style, atmosphere and way of life. They are gradually imposing a uniformity that was never there before. They are giving Cape Town a certain anonymity and destroying its personality and intimate flavour. It is happening not only to Cape Town, but to all large cities, for modern architecture is no longer Italian or Spanish or American. It is international. Cities all over the world are looking more and more alike. Only those that manage to keep their essential character and retain memories of their past, will continue to be a unique and worthwhile experience.

It would, however, be unfair to blame everything on modern architecture. Those tall new buildings are perhaps the most obvious symbols of change, and if they appear too jarring and assertive we should remember perhaps that like modern art they are only a reflection of modern society. There are many other things that have changed Cape Town and, in my opinion, impoverished the life of the city.

The laws of the land and various municipal ordinances have had their effect. There has been the submission of the local authorities to the mass assault on this city of the motor-car. And the car has won and will go on winning. There has been the virtual destruction of District Six which has also changed the character of Cape Town. The spirit of free enterprise which once filled Cape Town with innumerable small shops and other businesses has been crushed by monopolies like the supermarkets.

A most incredibly silly star-rating system has put scores of charming little hotels out of business; places that offered a visitor all he ever wanted: a clean room, a hot bath or shower and a good simple meal. With them have gone many of South Africa's most delightful pubs. Many of them had swing doors opening onto the streets, nearly all of them places of great warmth and conviviality. Their disappearance has all but put an end to a most colourful aspect of Cape Town life which produced an extraordinary array of characters for which Cape Town pubs were once famous.

In the cleaning-up process the local authorities also forced the hawkers and fruit vendors off the streets, another contribution to the dehumanizing of the city, and as far as I can remember the Coon Carnival, the only really vital, spontaneous and worthwhile festival South Africa has ever known, was discreetly diverted to a more suitable venue.

After all this it is incredible that Cape Town still has any charm left. I think it has. Buildings have a way of maturing as they grow older. Perspectives change and fashions change. Concepts of beauty also change. With eighteenth century Cape Town practically non-existent, nineteenth century Cape Town is now gaining favour. Many of those ornate Victorian buildings, regarded as tasteless not so long ago, have acquired an air of respectability and "atmosphere" of their own. In many cases restoration and a few coats of paint have proved that ornamentation is quaint and even charming. More important, many of these buildings stand in complexes and as a body of architecture they are our most substantial link with the past, and should be preserved.

If Cape Town is not going to change out of all recognition in the next twenty years, then people must show that they care. There must be a revaluation of what is left. If it is going to be a city for people then our streets must be places of activity, contact, communication and diversity as they were not so long ago. The best economic use possible must be made of old buildings worth saving. This is their only chance of survival.

The Trauma

ALL OF a sudden the mood of a city can change and it is often an upheaval of some kind that changes it. A city gives the people who live in it a sense of security, a feeling of certainty. It always confronts them with the familiar. They arrive in town by car, bus or train every day and walk the same way to their place of work. It is the assurance of the familiar that makes us do this. We pass the same shops, the same buildings, often we greet the same faces. They are all still there and everything is right with the world. Which is why we are shocked when suddenly the familiar is taken away and we are confronted with something new in its place, often something so assertive (in the case of a modern building) that it creates an entirely new atmosphere.

In Cape Town over the last fifteen years the destruction of the familiar has been a continuous process. Streets have been filled with dust and the air has been rent with noise. All this has been jarring on the nerves and it has changed our mood. We are not as friendly as we used to be, we have become insecure, irritable and, like many of our new buildings, assertive. I can't remember exactly when we began to change because it was an accumulative process, but I am prepared to bet that it all began in the mid-1960s. It was then, for the first time, that the unhappy truth began to dawn on Capetonians. A new kind of violence, operating under the cloak of progress and economic prosperity, began to turn the centre of their city into mounds of rubble and dust, and new gleaming edifices began to rise from the old.

Cape Town people are on the whole kind and tolerant. They have a touching loyalty to their city, they will always love it no matter how ugly it grows and they will never choose to live anywhere else. They have a quiet faith that as long as the mountain is there, nothing will go wrong. They know that the developers will never be able to move it.

Like most traditional communities, they are suspicious of change, but when it is forced on them they will, in time, accept it and eventually absorb it into their own pattern of life even if it causes them anguish. Vociferous or violent protest is not in their nature, they would rather keep their feelings to themselves. But there are times when they can be moved to behave in the strangest manner and this often happens when their curiosity is aroused.

Stand at a street corner and keep looking up towards the sky and you will soon have scores of Capetonians looking up with you. No-one will think of asking you what you are looking at; Capetonians have a tradition of minding their own business. They will simply assume that it must be something out of the ordinary. Let a gang of municipal workers dig a hole in Greenmarket Square and in no time there will be a gang of Capetonians watching them. This probably happens in other cities too, but in Cape Town people seem to be addicted to this kind of thing. It might well be that they get rid of their frustrations that way. And in recent years they have been deeply frustrated by the violence that has been done to their city because they haven't had much say in the matter.

There was one place which was always very close to their hearts – the old Fletcher and Cartwright Building at the corner of Darling Street and Adderley Street. Known as Cartwright's Corner, it was by far the city's most popular meeting place.

When the news spread that this loved landmark was to be demolished to make way for a concrete skyscraper, people realized for the first time that something was happening to the city which was beyond their comprehension and control. They knew that when the bulldozers moved in on Cartwright's Corner they would experience a traumatic break with the past, with the romantically familiar.

Within about eight months their worst fears were confirmed. A high scaffolding had been erected round Cartwrights and the demolition began. Within a matter of months this famed corner of Cape Town was reduced to an enormous hole in the ground. It was a humiliation we have never forgotten.

The hole was a turning point in the post-war history of Cape Town and I for one am convinced that it, and other holes like it, have had a profound psychological effect on the citizenry. Over a period of months, thousands of people were drawn to it as if magnetized and they stood and stared at it in silent anguish before moving away.

Whether there was some Freudian symbolism in the attraction is not for me to say, but after studying the behaviour of the hole-watchers for some weeks I believe that there might have been. The point is that there were growing numbers of ordinary, sane people, many of standing in the community, who couldn't keep away from it. They were people of all races. Mostly they kept their thoughts to themselves, but if they happened to catch your eye they would shake their heads. Among them were a number of professional men and businessmen. A regular visitor was a judge of the Supreme Court. Soon a special viewing platform was erected to accommodate the hundreds of sad-faced watchers.

A curious symptom of the syndrome was that people never talked or had any communication with one another. There was nothing but a bewildered silence. Their faces were dead pan, disconcertingly expressionless, but sometimes fleeting looks of nostalgia intruded on the contemplative silence. They were like mourners.

It was something that fascinated me and I questioned other hole-watchers whenever I had the opportunity. An estate agent who confessed his indignation at the destruction of the old building, said he first went to the site to see how great the destruction was. As soon as he started looking down into the hole it exerted a strange morbid influence on him and he had visited it every day since. A middle-aged bank manager said he visited the hole to confirm his own theories of what was happening to the city. Whenever the blasting began he dropped everything and went over as fast as he could.

An accountant whose office in Adderley Street overlooked the site, said he felt that in a way he was watching a symbolic burial. But he was also interested in the huge constructional problems that the hole presented. He liked working them out in his own mind, just as some people liked working out crossword puzzles. A dental mechanic who used to have lunch at Cartwrights every day of the week confessed that he had aggressive feelings towards the hole. He went and looked at it every day in the hope that something disastrous would happen.

Meanwhile, I had become a dedicated hole-watcher myself and visited it at least once a day and sometimes twice. I found that staring down into it had a soothing effect on me. Somehow the sheer magnitude of the task facing the workers down there made one's ordinary mundane problems appear insignificant. Out of interest I asked a well-known city psychiatrist to comment on the hole-watching phenomenon. What motivated all those people who spent so much time watching a mere excavation? Naturally he couldn't answer the question unless he knew the motives of each hole-watcher, but he was disturbed about the development of Cape Town himself and he didn't rule out the possibility that people visiting the site were moved by feelings of resentment and nostalgia. They could have been attending a symbolic burial of a way of life that had passed away for ever.

After a couple of weeks another significant thing happened. A hole-watcher behind me tapped me on the shoulder and accused me of jumping the queue. Worse still he told me that the place I was standing at on the platform was the spot he usually occupied. Such behaviour would have been unheard of in Cape Town of the pre-excavation era.

The hope that my own involvement with the hole would be dispassionate and objective turned out to be illusory. Soon I was mentally and emotionally beaten up and the progress of my addiction will remain with me for ever, clearly and hauntingly.

Firstly, it is necessary to appreciate the sense of awe and confusion with which the lay mind saw the Adderley Street operation. The hole was a dizzy depression hewn and blasted out of solid rock. Men working in it looked like helmeted insects moving about in a concrete canyon. In the main excavation there were other holes big enough to accommodate a double-decker bus.

Scattered about in deliberate and intricate confusion were the thousands of steel bars which would reinforce the steadily rising multiple layers of concrete. There were hoists, bastions, cranes, cement-mixers, pipes, beams, hoses, pumps, mouldings, shuttering, blasting equipment, barrels, buckets and tools: a confusion made more confusing by the reverberating, blasphemous clatter of pneumatic drills. This jarring sound accompanied by the deep thud of pile-drivers, echoed through the streets of Cape Town, as if telling everyone to get ready for the brave new world to come. The noise was hardly food for the soul. And there seemed to be thousands of pieces in the jigsaw puzzle, all waiting to find some place in this grimly growing structure of staggering complexity. It was so big that no-one could grasp it. Onlookers were dumbfounded. It told you that Cape Town had finally entered the technological age. The old was going for good. The hole proved it. And everyone you spoke to agreed.

At the same time the confusion was one of the things that fascinated: how would the ordered growth of a new city emerge from such vast chaos? Who decided what pipes went where? How did that giant crane get there and how the hell would they ever get it out? Such questions became part of the total distraction.

I am not alone in believing that mutilations such as this one, and others perpetrated elsewhere in the city, generated an anxiety neurosis that spread to many people. Mostly it was an anxiety about the future and the fact that something people had always relied on could be swept away so swiftly and ruthlessly and that an entirely new environment could be created in its place. Trusted values had no permanency any more. A new life-style, a new mode of behaviour, even new concepts of beauty and worth were arriving with the new towers of steel and concrete.

Cape Town as everyone knew it, was vanishing.

Junk, Bells and Pageantry

THERE is so much of Cape Town vanishing before our eyes that it is reassuring to visit the Grand Parade and get the feel of its permanence. It's amazing how this large stretch of open ground, bare and often windswept, has acquired an atmosphere which is typically Cape Town. There are no buildings, yet it has this feeling of history about it, probably because so much has happened on the Parade, so many great events have taken place here. It has seen soldiers going to war, it has acclaimed kings and presidents and it has been the place where great crowds have gathered to affirm or protest. But even events such as these are not its real secret, which to me lies in the rich and varied human activity we see on the Parade any Saturday morning.

It is Cape Town at its best. Hundreds of people converge on the Parade from every part of the Peninsula to swell the crowds of bargain hunters and raise the volume of conversation, people of every race and colour bartering and bargaining in every South African language and dialect. The stalls of the open air market are always laden with merchandise of every conceivable description. One wonders where it all comes from. Much of it is junk. The extraordinary thing is that eventually, everything – down to the last bent teaspoon – finds a buyer. Among the crowds flocking round the laden trestle tables you will always find one or two established collectors. Their eyes and noses are sharply attuned to anything that looks like a genuine antique or an item of Africana. If they are lucky they will occasionally find real bargains for a song. A collector I know bought a set of blackened spoons for fifty cents. They turned out to be real silver.

I always imagined that eventually people would get tired of the market on the Parade, that the stall-holders themselves would give up and pack up. But on a recent visit one sunny winter morning most of the old faces were still there and they still had old items of brass, pewter, china and copper which, I am sure, were there ten years ago, unless of course there is a constant supply of such bric-à-brac from auction sales, old homes and deceased estates. And there were as many buyers as ever. One stall was laden with the most unbelievable collection of junk and when I asked the stall holder whether he would ever sell any of it he said: "Of course, every cracked bit of it. Somewhere, sometime, somehow there will be a buyer for everything. There is nothing here that someone will not find some use for sometime. All I have to do is wait."

Already there was an African offering 10 cents for a broken meat mincer. On my right a learned-looking man in spectacles paid 5 cents for a battered copy of Witgenstein's *Tractatus*, an old spinsterish woman bought a bent wire lampshade for 1 c and a Coloured man was saying that he would buy an engine block if it didn't cost more than R5. He got it for even less.

Looking at all those tables bending under the weight of an incredible variety of goods was like taking a glance at a huge index of human activity. Every item seemed to tell a story. At one stall I made a list of the goods offered as my eye caught them: speedometers, pendants, ties, socks, 78 rpm records, Parlophone needles "scientifically made – extra loud," shoes, handbags, hairpins, wigs, electric heaters, nuts, bolts, brackets, electric fittings, a blow torch, gas cylinders, needle threaders, baskets, radio parts, pulleys, tin foil buttons, jampot lids, a set of drums, a wash-basin, dresses, a fire brigade hose, two old telephones, a car battery, and a man in the crowd wearing half-moon glasses saying to the delight of everyone: "I'm looking for something I cannot find." "Here it is mister," said a sharp-witted salesman holding up an ornate Victorian chamber pot, "and you can have it for R5."

There was still more to amuse and delight: old photograph albums, china, brassware, ash trays, opera glasses, silver candelabra, a brass Buddha, a toaster, fly swatters, egg beaters, car batteries, old bottles, mirrors, sea shells, clocks including a grandfather, swords, glassware, earthenware, crockery, lace, linen, African masks, a zebra skin and the stuffed foot of an ostrich.

At a neighbouring stall there was a pile of broken and rusted machinery, a box of old tools, war medals and ribbons, an oval picture of *The Laughing Cavalier*, a scale calibrated from one to eight ounces for weighing letters, vases, cups, trophies and brass miniatures.

I stopped at a table piled up with old 78 rpm gramophone records which you could buy with an old HMV wind-up gramophone. I wound it up and it worked and the man put on a record for me: Louis "Satchmo" Armstrong singing in his gravelly voice, "I'm gonna kill you just for fun".

I browsed through the old 78 records: Fritz Kreisler playing "Caprice Vienneise" and "Humoresque", Heifitz playing "On wings of song", Marek Weber and his orchestra playing "Carmen", the Queen's Hall Orchestra conducted by Sir Henry Wood playing "Danse Macabre" and "Immortal Strauss".

The Parade has always had its share of loafers, cranks and pickpockets. It still has its fanatical preachers with their warnings of fire and brimstone and their promises of salvation. I can remember one man telling us quite emphatically that the world was going to end within a year unless it repented. That was at least ten years ago. I don't know where he got his message from, but quite obviously he had been misinformed. I never saw him on the Parade again. But about three years ago during the lunch hour, he was sounding off in Greenmarket Square. He was certainly a man of tremendous conviction because he was saying the same thing all over again.

In 1928 a man set up a small photographic stall on the Parade with equipment which was then hopelessly out of date. He had an open-air studio consisting of a couple of chairs and a square of painted canvas as a background. His camera was an old wooden box with a sleeve at the end of it. It was held together by leather straps. Near the camera he kept a bucket of water, a developer stand made of boxwood, and a crude glass display case in which he exhibited his work. Over the years he made a lot of money, trading on sentimentality. He took photographs of boys and girls for their sweethearts, of sons for their mothers and of soldiers for their folks back home. The head of the loved one would be framed in a heart or a horseshoe with a dove of peace perched on top, accompanied by a few lines of dreadfully sentimental verse. The old-time photographer retired last year and sold all his equipment to the man who runs the show now. But the camera which was old fifty years ago is still in use and business on Saturday mornings is booming.

Dora Maritz is one of the herb-sellers who has a stall beneath the palm trees, facing Darling Street. She has a steady sale of her herbs and people of all races buy them to ease their pains or cure their ailments. She doesn't like doctors and has no patience with people who question her motives. She recommends buchu for rheumatism, Hottentot kwygoed for "asthma and heart", wilde dagga for "sugar and high blood", khakibossie or wildeknoffel for the lungs, wildepatat for the stomach and kameelbol for piles, which just about covers everything.

The early history of the Parade began soon after Van Riebeeck built the fort. It was probably here where Van Riebeeck had his market garden. The building of the Castle began in 1666, but it wasn't till about 1740 that slaves were used to level the ground which the Parade now occupies. It was given a border of shrubs and trees. Fashionable people of the day used to take their walks here. There is a grim side to its history too. A gallows was erected on the far side near the Castle and people were tortured and executed in public.

The Parade has always been there and the fact that it has largely been left untouched has given it a quality of certainty. But it is doubtful whether it will always be there. It is one of the places whose use must be evaluated. Already it has been turned into a car park and there have been rumours of moves to use this large open space more economically.

Overlooking it is the City Hall and these two established landmarks seem to complement each other: the Parade providing the space which gives the City Hall its commanding appearance. It is far more than just the civic heart of Cape Town; over the years it has become the symbol of sanity and tolerance, keeping its doors open to all of its citizens at all times as long as it was allowed to do so by law.

So much has happened in the City Hall that there are few people who do not feel that it means something to them: meetings of all kinds, exhibitions, celebrations, balls, banquets, sports events, concerts, ballets, operas. Indeed there were times when the City Hall carried the cultural life of Cape Town and South Africa on its shoulders, especially the country's musical life.

Although its many functions will soon be transferred to the new civic centre on the foreshore, the City Hall will continue for a very long time to be the emotional heart of Cape Town, for it has imprinted itself on the City's conscience. There appears to be some doubt about its future function. One thing is certain: it must be made useful otherwise we will be in danger of losing it. It would make an admirable cultural centre. It could become the permanent home of the Cape Town Symphony Orchestra and its minor halls could be used for exhibitions of all kinds. Its whole style and mood lends itself to such a purpose. Built in the Italian Renaissance style, it has some marvellous ornamentation, with

Mr Wellington Parade photographer

columns, pilasters, pediments, balustrades and a fine frieze with the city's coat of arms in the middle.

It would be a great pity too if it was wholly deserted by the City Council. There is one ceremony above all, with all its pomp and ceremony, that couldn't possibly be held anywhere else without losing its dignity, and this is the inauguration of a new Mayor.

This installation ceremony is about all the pageantry that is left in Cape Town and my fear is that if it is transferred to any other atmosphere, it will begin to look ridiculous and eventually vanish, and Cape Town will have lost another traditional splash of colour in its civic life. Already it is in danger of dying out because so few people are able to witness it. Perhaps television will bring its glories to a wider audience.

These pageants certainly give one a new insight into the meaning of mayorship, for one realizes right away why so many of our mayors take themselves and their office so seriously. It's the installation ceremony that does it. All the tradition that suddenly bears down upon them seems to increase the air pressure by several pounds per square inch, so it must have a deep effect on mere mortals like incoming mayors, infusing them with a crushing sense of mission and responsibility.

The last installation ceremony I attended was a resplendent affair with a great sense of occasion heightened by all the traditional trappings that the City Hall could muster: insignia, bright robes, uniforms, flowers, lights, celebrities and courtly seventeenth century music. There was a man up among the organ pipes with a long beard like Johannes Brahms, giving a spirited rendering of the "Allegra Deciso" from Handel's Water Music, going at it so furiously that you wondered how he could handle the pedals, the notes and the stops all at the same time.

It was stirring, optimistic music for a joyous ceremony and somehow it gave a fairytale atmosphere to the proceedings. The seats behind the stage were heavily banked with shrubbery supplied no doubt, by the Parks and Gardens Department. Peeping out were the silky faces of flowers, and here and there little fountains of daffodils threw up yellow sprays. The stage itself was enlarged into an impressive oval, heavily carpeted in yellow. In the centre stood the Chair of Van Riebeeck, tall and stern, the throne of all Cape Town mayors, and behind it a large replica of the City's coat-of-arms. And on each side of it were lesser chairs for the Deputy Mayor and Town Clerk.

On the extreme flanks sat important guests and other luminaries, with more shrubbery in the background dotted with sparks of yellow and red carnations. The huge yellow carpet even covered the floor below the stage where more chairs were suitably arranged for the councillors and the heads of the various municipal departments.

Among the serried ranks of guests, celebrities were dotted about like jewels in a cavern: the gold braid of admirals, the red and blue epaulets of high-ranking officers, archbishops in their purple stocks and behind them lower ranks of clergy. And there were judges, Members of Parliament, various other grey and balding figures of local fame and, wafting in and out, some very expensive scents emanating from the bodies of some very expensive women.

How the Van Riebeeck Chair became part of all the City Hall's tradition is still something of a mystery. No-one seems to know why it is called the Van Riebeeck Chair in the first place. It seems unlikely that Van Riebeeck himself ever sat on it because its feet are machine-made, indicating more recent origins; unless, of course, the present feet were added later. Anyway it's an impressive chair by any standards, and the seat is so high that short mayors usually find themselves seated on this throne with their feet dangling above the floor. This, if it was noticed by the public, could detract from the dignity of their office, but the maker of the chair never thought of that. Happily one normally never sees where their feet are, so the chair retains its look of authority. It has been said that not even a mouse could sit in it without feeling a surge of power.

The happenings at mayoral installations are timed to the second. Just when one has taken in all the surrounding splendour, the music takes on a more sombre note and the proceedings begin to move. Enter the councillors all draped in black-and-blue robes, all looking like ex-mayors or mayors yet to be and led in solemn file by the most senior among them, in this case the venerable A. Z. Berman who has since died, but was then the doyen and grandfather of all City Fathers.

Very conscious they all seemed of the importance of the occasion and they moved as slowly and gravely as a procession of condemned men, manacled by their robes. No-one would have been surprised if they had launched into the "Prisoner's Chorus" from *Fidelio*. Thankfully they didn't. Thankfully they all reached their seats and everything was now set for the important business of the day, the changing over from the old Mayor, Mr F. M. Friedlander, to the new ascendant, Mr David Bloomberg.

We were not kept waiting long. Suddenly the Brahmsian beard up there among the organ pipes turned itself into a small hairy whirlwind and the whole hall resounded with a sort of heraldic fanfare that must have shaken the entablature of the City Hall's stone façade. Inside, the rafters seemed to shake and a frightened bird flew out of a fanlight window.

Mr Friedlander always looked the typical Mayor, but when he entered from a side door in his bright red robes trimmed with blue and gold, he looked the part to perfection. Following him was Mr David Bloomberg and the Town Clerk in his black robes and curled silver wig. Leading them was a bald, solemn-faced man in livery, bearing the Mayor's traditional symbol of authority, the Mace, as if it was an executioner's axe.

Mr Friedlander, florid, rotund and majestic, had no need of symbols. He looked the very essence of authority himself, with his gilt chain of office gleaming, the round medallion resting comfortably on his comfortable-looking solar plexus. If he'd worn a moustache, small beard and a velvet hat lined with ermine he would have looked just like Henry VIII, a happy Henry, a portly chunk of amiability. For here was a man who had done a fine job and enhanced the prestigious office. It was no wonder that he oozed a kind of bountiful *bonhomie*, generously returning smiles in all directions. He filled the Chair of Van Riebeeck as if it had been made for him, and it is a very large chair.

He made his speech as out-going Mayor in ringing tones, with microphones perched round his head like attentive birds, and after he had reviewed the work of the year and thanked just about everybody for just about everything, the Town Clerk got up and called on him and his Deputy-Mayor to surrender the keys of the Common Seal of the Council. This they obligingly did. Then the Mayor called for nominations for his successor and up into the breach and to the microphone stepped Mr Walter Gradner, a tried and true councillor if ever there was one. And what Mr Gradner said made one realize that history was, in fact, repeating itself.

He recalled that more than twenty-five years earlier his father who had once been Mayor, Mr Louis Gradner (known in his time as Louis the Boss) had nominated Mr David Bloomberg's father (the one and only Abe). And now he, the son of Louis the Boss, was nominating David, the son of Abe. It almost sounded like a nice family business.

It must be mentioned, of course, that Mr Walter Gradner himself was also the Mayor at some time or other and so was Mr Gerry Ferry who now stepped up to another microphone to second the nomination, after which everyone realized that one Mayor was about to be exchanged for another. Mr David Bloomberg was in fact declared elected and, accompanied by his sponsors, Mr Friedlander and the Town Clerk, he left the hall to be invested with his robes and insignia of office.

It seemed as if this part of the ritual had to be done as quickly as possible. As with monarchs there had to be continuity – a case of "The King is dead, long live the King", except that here it was a case of: one Mayor has had his time, wheel on another.

That beard among the organ pipes now turned into a tornado and the blast of the fanfare that heralded the entrance of the new Mayor did more than just shake the rafters. It was thunderous. This time a whole lot of birds flew out of fanlight windows. Dust rose from the uncarpeted part of the floor. The walls seemed to shake and guests shifted uneasily in their seats, as if hoping for one of those helmets workers wear on building sites. But the old City Hall held firm and, launched on this huge contrapuntal wave of sound, Cape Town's newest and youngest Mayor, robed and chained in red and gold, made his way to the throne, led once again by the terribly worried man in livery whose white socks below his knee breeches made him look remarkably like a maribou stork.

But even before Mr Bloomberg reached the throne he looked like a man to whom authority came easily: smooth, self-controlled, alert, intelligent. He looked completely at home in his mayor's robes, almost as if he'd been rehearsing the part in the Barn Theatre for the last few years. When he finally took his seat in the Chair of Van Riebeeck, one couldn't help feeling that a fresh new wind was beginning to blow from the City Hall. The stork in knee-breeches, now looking almost as if he'd lost the baby, handed him the Key of the Common Seal on a blue velvet cushion which was even better than handing it to him on a plate.

With this last symbol of office in his possession and very much in possession of himself, the new Mayor made his speech. An impressive effort it was too. Here was a man who knew exactly what he wanted, knew where he was going and the shortest way to get there.

When last did Cape Town hear the bells of the City Hall carillon? I don't pretend to know. The great instrument is still there in the clock tower, but its festive music seems to be a thing of the past. As far as I know, the bells have been silent since 1963 and the silent bells await a maestro, someone who can play them, a carilloneur. Carilloneurs were much in demand once, but times have changed. The music they make might be beautiful, but there are few people today who want to hear it, they haven't the patience and they haven't got the time. In any case, the sound of the bells would be drowned by the noise of Cape Town's traffic.

I got onto fairly intimate terms with the carillon about twelve years ago when Mr Jan Luyt was Town Clerk. He was a big, jovial man with a generous heart, but he was never sure that his heart was in the right place. He was a good, conscientious Town Clerk, but I always got the feeling that his heart was up in the City Hall clock tower with the thirty-nine bells of the carillon. He was one of the last people who loved the instrument and knew how to play it. The day I called on him and asked about the bells he dropped everything else and insisted on taking me high up into the clock tower.

He couldn't wait to get at the bells and, stripping down to his braces, he sat at the huge keyboard and began bashing away at the wooden keys with his fists (that's how the carillon is played) and shifting up and down the music bench like a demon as he attacked the base notes with his feet. Any carillon player is sunk unless he can use his feet. It is hard work. Even practising a few scales makes you puff, so you have to be pretty fit to do the job.

Jan Luyt went at it with a kind of devotional frenzy, like a modern J. S. Bach whipping up a little something for posterity. You just couldn't get him away from those bells. I dare say that if it wasn't that he had to attend some committee meeting, he would have stayed up in the murky bell-tower all afternoon and insisted on me staying with him.

The carillon as a musical instrument has been going through lean times. There are not many people left who give it a passing thought. As far as I know there is no-one in Cape Town who can play it or who wants to play it – with the possible exception of Mr Keith Jewell. Unless a new carilloneur comes to light in the near future the song of the beautiful bells might never be heard again.

Like piano tuners, carilloneurs are becoming a dying breed, for a man who plays the bells must not only be a good musician, he must have those spiritual qualities of tolerance, meekness and self-denial. In fact he must be something of a saint. Only then can he inherit Cape Town's carillon. He must love the instrument in a Platonic sort of way without ever wanting to possess it. It is much too big to carry away. It is a permanent fixture up there in the bell-tower of the City Hall. Perhaps this is why people don't take up the carillon any more. It is so much more convenient to take up the violin or guitar – at least you can carry them around with you. Not the carillon. It weighs ten tons. The biggest bell weighs two tons.

Many musicians today live on adulation. To say the least, it's one of their main sources of nourishment. I don't think they would be able to survive spiritually without that roar of applause that engulfs them at the end of a piano or lieder recital. The carilloneur has to do without this. That's where the quality of meekness comes in. He never sees his audience and they never see him high up there in the clock tower. He must be able to produce real virtuoso stuff without hearing a single clap or a call for an encore. No praise, no bouquets and no curtain calls for him. This alone makes his job an anachronism in an age of super stardom.

Nevertheless, being a carillon player has its advantages. Maybe it is only the trombone player who can afford to let things slide, but it is only the carilloneur who can afford to bash away and probably get rid of a lot of aggression in the process. According to Jan Luyt, when I spoke to him that afternoon up in the bell-tower, the more you bash away the more you like it. The thing grows on you. The beautiful melodious peal of the bells gets you, and eventually the very sight of them becomes visible music.

If this does not impress, then there is another inducement for the prospective carillon player. There is always the chance of him composing a few masterpieces for the instrument and gaining his place among the immortals of music. Very little music has been written for the carillon and the repertoire consists mainly of arrangements from the classics. Even then all the music must be transcribed to bring it within the compass of three octaves.

The carillon's history is a solid and worthy one. The instrument dates back to the sixteenth century and it was first played in Belgium and Holland. Roundabout the seventeenth century it went into the doldrums, but made a big come-back 100 years later. Cape Town's bells were made in England and installed sixty years ago. They were first played by Anton Brees, a carilloneur from Belgium, when the Prince of Wales visited South Africa in 1925.

Jan Luyt was Brees's pupil and was carilloneur for many years before Walter Piper, a member of the City Orchestra, took his place. Walter Piper died about twenty-three years ago and Ian Vermaak, a carilloneur from Holland, took over. But he resigned to take another job and the bells have been silent ever since, although they might have made a sporadic comeback now and then.

The sound of the bells means something to surviving relatives and friends of those who died in World War I. They are in fact, war memorials. Each bell is dedicated to a brigade, a regiment, or groups of men who sacrificed their lives. One bears the names of all the municipal employees who never came back. Their magical sound, if we ever hear them again, will be a memory of the dead.

District Six

I WALKED up to District Six the other day to see how much of it has been cleared away. A little of it remains, but the whole area between Canterbury Street and Russell Street is starkly empty with only a public lavatory and an old stone church still standing, guarding the spirit of the past. Most of the mountain side of Hanover Street has been torn away, but the Seven Steps where the old Globe Gang used to meet in the late 1940s are still there, so is the Fish Market, so is St Mark's Church and the old Moravian Church.

In Muir Street, the mosque with its coat of mustard-yellow paint shines among the surrounding ruins like a great star; near by the Aspling Street Mosque with its decorative tower has been given a new coat of paint. The municipal wash-house is still there in Clifton Street and so is the service kitchen in Canterbury Street. But the planned destruction has been enormous and the heart of the place has just about stopped beating.

Anyone who knew District Six as it was cannot stand among the flattened ruins without feeling the impoverishment Cape Town has suffered by this unimaginable loss. It has been far more than the city can afford. It was a university of racial harmony. When authority decided to uproot and disperse this community, they switched off an oven of contentment and goodwill. Much of District Six was a slum, there was a great deal of poverty, but there was a community spirit that the most advanced urban development will never be able to buy or replace, a spirit which profoundly influenced race relations in the Peninsula. District Six was one of the poorest communities in Cape Town, but it was unquestionably the gayest and happiest. Its children had many homes and many mothers and fathers. Amid all the smells and deprivation there was one thing they were never deprived of – love and emotional security.

Sociologists know now that massive slum clearance destroys a valuable social and street life as well as a community spirit which can never be re-established in a new housing scheme. Slum clearance by removal is sweeping away poverty at the cost of stability and social cohesion, there is a loss of mutual support and an increase in lawlessness and antisocial behaviour.

One cannot help recalling District Six as the vital, effervescent, exuberant place it was only a few years ago before it became Cape Town's punctured lung. In spite of the slums, the crowded conditions, the shebeens, the skollies, it was a living example of human harmony. A way of life had evolved in which Whites, Coloureds, Indians, Moslems, Christian, Jew, Upper Class, Middle Class, Lower Class and no class at all lived and worked together without racial friction.

The D.R.C. Mission Church stood tolerantly beside a mosque a few metres away. It was not merely a district, but a completely self-contained town with its own very special character; its way of life highly organized and traditional. Its people were always very much aware of this. Emotionally they were deeply involved with the dilapidated but quaint environment that produced them. Not a single person I ever spoke to wanted to leave.

Economically, District Six used to be inseparable from Cape Town. On any Saturday morning you could see thousands of shoppers steaming down Hanover and Caledon streets into the centre of the city. They used to flock into the shops, bazaars and delicatessens between Buitenkant Street and Adderley Street. Many of the furniture shops on the main road between Woodstock and Salt River relied heavily on District Six for their custom.

It was not only a large and reliable source of labour, but one of the main distribution points in the Peninsula for the agricultural produce of the Cape. Farmers knew that they could send their lorry-loads of fruit and vegetables there at any time of the day or night and get their price in cash. From there the produce found its way into thousands of Peninsula homes from Simonstown to Sea Point.

District Six, with its predominantly Moslem population was one of the homes of the Afrikaans language. Afrikaans was spoken in most homes. While the Koran is printed in Arabic, all other literature on Moslem custom and practice is in Afrikaans. The people proudly claimed that they were one of the staunchest guardians of the language and one of the great influences from District Six that found its way into Afrikaans writing was the spicey grain of its humour. Afrikaans poets, among them Uys Krige, gladly took up the beat of its rhythms, its song and dance as silk-clad, fiery columns of Coons swarmed out of that hive like bees.

The place had more barber shops to the acre than any other town on earth and almost as many tailors. There were all kinds of alleys and lanes with names like Rotten Row, Drury Lane and Lavender Hill. Only the names are still there. There were herbalists, grocers, butchers, tattoo artists, curry shops, clothing stores, cinemas, bars, public wash-houses and people engaged in every conceivable activity. But what mattered was the people, their sense of belonging, their high spirits and irrepressible sense of humour. Their haunting faces with the lines and shades of just about every human type on earth: European, African, Arabic, Oriental, Semitic, Hottentot – all blending with one another, but each somehow retaining some vestige of its origins.

The hawkers with their barrows at nearly every street corner, piled with pyramids of fruit and vegetables. The fish market with snoek, katonkel and Cape salmon gleaming on cold marble slabs. The men in dark alleys, the young girls threatening you with their sex appeal, the skollies and Fah-fee runners, the loafers, the cripples, the drunks, men in smart suits wearing dark glasses and red or black fezzes, here and there an Imam in his Moslem robes and children everywhere like busy insects.

District Six was one of the world's most exciting meeting grounds of people of many religions, colours and races, and its great contribution was that it proved that none of these things really mattered. It was one of the few realities in South Africa. It had dirty gutters, broken windows, peeling walls, dirty windows, slummy backyards, and in places, an oily griminess. But it had honesty. No man or woman who lived there ever tried to be anything but what he was. There was no hypocrisy and everyone knew where he stood, knew what he was likely to get out of life and what was beyond his reach. Its people clung to it physically and spiritually. Often it was a place of violence, but mostly it was a place of love. There was poverty, but there was kindness and its people understood that the only meaning life has, is the meaning one gives to it.

District Six always had two faces and it was a tragedy that in the end it was judged by its outward face, the obvious face, the face of the slum. No-one cared about the hidden face behind those dismal doors. Behind the cracked and sordid façades were some of the best-kept homes in the Peninsula and some of the happiest. This was the great paradox and also one of the tragedies of District Six.

It was a situation that came about over many years because of landlords who took everything out of District Six and put nothing back. With the profits from their rents they invested elsewhere in more valuable areas, but they hardly spent a cent maintaining the dwellings that gave them the profits. A few realized their obligations and kept some houses in good shape. But most didn't keep their part of the bargain. The tenant undertook to maintain the inside of the house; the landlord had to look after the outside. One old woman whose family had lived in Hanover Street for 88 years told me that her landlord had not spent anything on the house for 40 years. She couldn't afford to do so, and eventually the dwelling gave every appearance of a slum. She had spent all her money maintaining the inside which was still immaculate.

Wherever one went in District Six one heard this story over and over again. It was the honest, hard-working man who spent years fighting for a decent kind of life and found it in his beloved District Six, who lost in the end.

Ten years ago you could find a character in District Six round every corner. Apart from the odd gang there were all kinds of strange activities and sub-cultures. A man who knew how to mesmerize a chicken could be as famous in his own little community as a man who'd made a lot of money. Poverty, of course, bred a lot of crime, but even a criminal who showed any special talent was admired, like the man who stole a large safe from a firm in Long Street by rolling it down the street on billiard balls. There used to be a beggar who was held in high regard because he could sit on a pavement in such a way that his legs below his knees were skilfully hidden from view and his knees looked like the stumps of a double amputation. The amazing stories he told about how he lost his legs earned him much sympathy and kept him in whiskey. He was a regular at the old Cheltenham Bar which at one time was run by Charlie Terblanche, a former detective who served sundowners to men he had once hunted down and arrested.

A man held in high esteem at the Cheltenham was a character called Harry Olympics, so called because when they let him out of jail he never stopped running – and he ran straight to the Cheltenham. But this wasn't why Harry Olympics was famous. His real claim to popular regard was that he could blow the fish horn louder than anyone else in the Peninsula – which was all the more remarkable because he was a small, wiry man who at one time had a spot on the lung. But when he blew the fish horn, the veins in his neck swelled up like balloons and his eyes became bloodshot. They said that on a quiet day you could hear him two miles away. He could even play tunes on it, but only his fans could recognize what they were. The volume he managed to get from the horn came from a secret way he held his mouth, a secret which he would only pass on to his eldest son, to keep the trick in the family.

Harry Olympics died before he could pass his secret on to anybody and since his death, the fish horn itself appears to have vanished from the Cape Town scene – which might be a good or a bad thing depending on what that extraordinary sound does to one's musical sensibilities. The horn had its origins many years ago with the kelp trumpet. Kolbe, a chronicler of life at the Cape many years ago, described the kelp ancestor of the fish horn as a native instrument called the "seaweed trumpet". When blown it resounded like the trumpeting of an elephant. For years, hawkers bringing their cart-loads of fish to Cape Town's suburbs announced their arrival on a fish horn. No housewife could mistake the mad, lowing sound, rather like the voice of a despairing cow. Most people couldn't stand it and the fish hawkers often raised the tempers of whole communities. On several occasions in the past there has been a public outcry against the horn and there have been demands that it should be banned. Such a protest was made in 1888; but the fish horn was still there at the turn of the century. A few years later, the following pompous petition was sent to the Mayor and Corporation of Cape Town: ". . . Ladies and gentlemen belonging to the musical, literary and theatrical world of Cape Town and suburbs ask that a law be passed prohibiting the appalling and terrible sound made by that barbaric instrument, the fish horn."

But the horn survived. However, in 1908 a visitor to the beautiful Cape protested against the fish horn in the following terms: "It may be objected that by long use, the blowers of the fish horns have a prescriptive right to make portions of the day and night hideous with their noises which not infrequently suggest the loud continuous creaking of an ill-greased cart wheel."

District Six was full of people who did the most unusual things for a living. In my wanderings through its narrow streets, I have met herbalists, quacks, tattooists, a polonymaker, a genuine shoemaker, a hatter, and a man who sold sandawana hairs for luck, "a bob each", and made a very good living out of them. The sandawana was supposed to be an African wolf, but was probably a strandwolf; there are no wolves in Africa. His line was that if you kept the hair under an armpit it would bring you safety, if you kept it in the groin it would bring you love and if placed behind the ear, wealth.

There was an old man who kept dozens of pairs of spectacles in a tray, reading glasses of all kinds, glasses for short sight, long sight, headaches and ordinary sun-glasses. He had scores of customers. You could take a pair of glasses home and try them. If they didn't improve your sight you could bring them back and take others. There were even a few monocles and pince-nez. None cost more than 2s. 6d. The old man was nearly blind himself, but he had a powerful magnifying glass which he would use to examine customers' eyes and tell them why they were "not looking too good".

I was lucky enough to have an interview with one of the last of the tattooists, a tall, sallow man with sleepy eyes who moved as if in a dream. He wore a white coat like a doctor and as we introduced each other he said, "Just call me Mr Adams." He was extremely dignified, if a little uneasy. Perhaps he was just anxious to explain that tattooing, one of the oldest crafts, really deserved the status of a profession. His place was in Hanover Street and he had done his best to make his office look like a doctor's waiting room. There were armchairs and a pile of old magazines on a round table. I gathered that he was one of the last two tattooists left in District Six. It was a dying trade in a materialistic age that no longer believed that certain signs and symbols on certain parts of the anatomy could bring you luck, wealth, love and sexual potency.

What was clear, however, was that there were, and still are, thousands of people in Cape Town, Black and White, male and female who have this irresistible, atavistic urge to have some symbolic sign decorating their bodies. They come from all tiers of society, from labourers to professional men, from prostitutes to women in high society. The only one noticeable difference: the more educated and sophisticated customers had more perverted ideas about what should be tattoed on their bodies and where – especially women.

But it wasn't easy to get Mr Adams to give any details. Like any "professional" he had a certain code of conduct. However, he was able to reveal that apart from the obvious fetishism which went with the desire to be tattooed, there were strong sexual associations. Customers had come to him with requests that had made him blush. For ethical reasons he had refused them, even when they had offered large sums of money.

Scores of women wanted certain symbols tattooed on various erotic parts of their bodies – between the breasts, inside the thighs, on the stomach and buttocks. Men had often wanted nipples tattooed on their buttocks and impressions of female lips on their torsos and thighs. There are tattoo marks that have a deep religious significance for some people, and others that are meant to be badges of courage, compassion and virtue. There are certain marks which brand the customer as a member of some gang or fraternity. Many criminals who have served jail sentences have five dots tattooed on their hands, four representing the four walls of the cell and the fifth, the prisoner inside the four walls. Dagga pedlars often have three dots tattooed on their arms and homosexuals also have certain identifying marks, so do lesbians and prostitutes.

There are hundreds of people in Cape Town who have had themselves tattooed for all sorts of reasons. Men who have lost their wives often want a cross with a scroll round it tattooed on their forearms. A popular sign with soldiers is a sword and scroll with some heroic catch phrase on it. One man had a bow tie tattooed round his neck and another who came out of Groote Schuur Hospital with an enormous operation scar across his abdomen, had the words tattooed across it: "Opened by mistake."

THE COFFIN

I had one of my most amusing and macabre experiences in District Six only a few years ago before the bulldozers moved in. It was an unbearably hot Saturday morning in February and the mountain was veiled in a heavy heat haze. Silent columns of smoke hung over the docks. It was windless and the slow shallow waves in the bay moved like muscles beneath a skin of blue silk. There were three of us: Frank Taylor, South Africa correspondent of the London Daily Telegraph, Cloete Breytenbach, the photographer, and myself. Our purpose was to show Taylor around the District. We drove up Hanover Street as far as the Crescent Restaurant and then we walked.

Everyone seemed to be out on the streets that day and the whole of Hanover Street was like a long trough of fermenting humanity: buses, cars, carts, hawkers with their piles of produce at the street corners, crying out their prices in competition with one another, hundreds of children darting in and out of the traffic, hooters, exclamations, oaths, shouts, laughter and a jostling of humanity that must have sent up the ambient temperature several degrees by body contact alone.

I had never before experienced such intense commotion, such raw smelly ebullience and fragrant effervescence. Every minute was a celebration of life itself, with voice and sweat and good humour. Washing hung over the railings and balconies like bunting. Kids jumped onto the platform of trams. Friends met on pavements, shook hands, slapped backs, walked on again. Pavements were too narrow, crowds spilled over into the street.

On the walls of a building, painted in red, were the words: "You are now in fairyland", and we might well have been. Everything and everybody seemed larger than life. Urchins tugged at shirts and held up the palms of their hands. An old man scolded them for begging and they ran away. We walked up Richmond Street with the flat stones hot and hard beneath our feet. The small houses on either side rose in terraces. The little stoeps with dwarf walls were piled with potted plants or bird cages, there were cats and dogs everywhere, excited children, shouting and darting about, playing with hoops, battered toys, broken dolls. A little boy came up and gave us a tune on a "trompie", doing a dance at the same time. Everyone thought it was a huge joke, and right the way up more washing was hanging over walls and stoeps and mothers were shrieking for their little ones.

We turned right down Ashley Street and stopped to look at the view of the veiled mountain and the lazy darkness over the bay. The heat was vibrant and visible. It was just about noon. On our left was the old Moravian Church with a wall in front and steps leading up to the twin front doors, both firmly closed. The church was a sudden square of silence in all the exhilarating confusion, a space of silence suddenly very strange.

But not for long. An old Peugeot van roaring up Richmond Street made a blistering turn into Ashley Street and bore down upon us with the driver's hand on the blaring horn. We jumped aside. The van accelerated past the Moravian Church and came to a tearing stop about twenty paces farther on. Doors slammed and two men got out on either side. One carried a bottle of white wine. He put it to his lips and drank it like water before handing what was left to his mate who drank the rest and tossed the bottle over the church wall.

As we passed they gathered themselves into attitudes of simulated sobriety. The one said "Happy New Year Master", and the other saluted us with palm and fingers spread all over his face. He wore a small straw hat with a porcupine quill in it and there was a dark toothless gap in his smile. The other wore a soft cap with the brim pushed up above a froglike face. Two sets of dark eyes, not very well focussed, explained their exaggerated bonhomie – both men were plastered. But they looked so beautifully irresponsible that you could not help liking them.

We walked on and they moved to the back of the van. There was a clatter of doors opening. There were curses and a sliding sound of something heavy being shifted and then there was a loud crash followed by an appallingly hoarse and disgusted voice saying: "Oo Here Padda, nou gan jy na die hell." At the same time he shouted to us: "Please master. Give us a hand ou pal!"

As we walked towards them they began to argue, with bitter accusations flying back and forth, but with neither giving way an inch. At their feet was a coffin they had pulled out of the van. In its fall it had come loose at the hinges. At first I couldn't understand why two grown men had not been able to take a coffin out of the van without dropping it. Then I realized that there was a body in it. In fact, it must have been a body of some considerable weight and size. It was an unusually large coffin, gleaming with varnish, brown, with silver handles.

It was an extraordinary moment. Suddenly the sweet smell of death had enveloped us with all its grief and loneliness, its everlasting silence. Here we were with two drunk men and a body. The presence of one dead person seemed to muffle all the clamour and noise of District Six. It was an anonymous body. No friends, no relatives. No wreaths or flowers. There was a small silver tablet on the coffin lid. On it was inscribed a name. It read simply: "Minnie Potts".

The man with the small straw hat was picking his teeth with the porcupine quill which he then broke nervously into small pieces. The man called Padda said they were looking for "the Reverend for the funeral". The body in the coffin was "the old girl we brought up from down the road in Caledon Street". No they were not drunk, they said, it was just that the coffin was too heavy and would the master please help carry it into the church.

Minnie Potts was heavy. The five of us carried her up the steps of the Moravian Church and laid her down before the door. The man in the small straw hat was called Mac. He walked round to the back of the church in search of "the Reverend". But the Moravian Church was closed and there was no sign of any Reverend. So Mac lit a cigarette and said that maybe they had brought the old girl to the wrong church. Which church were they looking for? Mac said they were looking for the "piskoppels", meaning the Episcopalian Mission. Well this was the Moravian. Okay, said Mac, would we mind looking after the Old Girl while they went and looked for the "Piskoppels".

We told him we were not prepared to wait more than a few minutes. And Mac said, okay Master, that was fine by him as long as we didn't mind. We did mind. As they walked towards the car they were unsteady on their feet. They got in, slammed the doors and tore away.

We decided, more out of curiosity than reverence, that we'd wait for quarter of an hour and then telephone the police. But it wasn't necessary. By now a crowd had gathered, mostly children staring at the coffin. The heat had become intolerable. We were feeling it and so was Minnie Potts. We moved away hoping for a breeze to spring up. Two men arrived and asked what all the trouble was about. We explained, and they said they'd send someone to find the Moravian minister so at least Minnie Potts could be inside the church and not out in the sun.

Everyone now stood clear of the coffin because of the heat. But then a young girl of about twelve pushed her way to the front and placed a plastic flower on top of the coffin. She appeared from nowhere. It was so sweetly done that everyone said "shame" and a woman began to cry. Yet no-one in the crowd knew who Minnie Potts was or anything about her, not even the young girl who had brought the plastic flower.

Then there was a terrible screech of car tyres and an engine revving and hooting. It was the Peugeot van again. It turned in from Richmond Street and came flying to a stop so that all the children gave way.

It was Mac and Padda, and you could almost smell the cheap wine as they got out of the car. Padda was now happy and doing a little *jol* on the pavement. Mac gave him a friendly clout and told him to have respect.

"The Reverend is waiting," Mac said, as he walked unsteadily up the steps. "If the Master will just help us put her back."

Again we lifted Minnie Potts, walked her down the steps of the Moravian Church and slid her coffin into the back of the Peugeot van. Mac and Padda jumped into the front seat and the doors slammed behind them. Padda grabbed a bottle from somewhere under the front seat and waved to the crowd as Mac accelerated and shot away with a roar of the engine and smoke coming from the tyres.

There were shouts of "shame, shame." The van disappeared round the far corner at what seemed like a godless speed.

And Minnie Potts was driven, we hoped, to her last resting place.

Malay Quarter

SOMEHOW the mood of the Malay Quarter is changing. The people are becoming withdrawn. You don't get the same spontaneous greeting from the children any more unless they are very young. Is it a defensive mood? I don't know. It could be that any community confined to a certain "quarter" behaves defensively.

I am not suggesting that the people in the quarter are unhappy. I think they're one of the happiest of communities. You can sense their pride in themselves and in their culture. They are a dignified people and they are aware of this. Once you get talking to them they are friendly and helpful, but you have to make the first move.

The Moslem butcher I talked to in Rose Street was a fierce little man with enormous hands. He was cutting away fat from a great leg of beef with a long sharp knife. His suspicious eyes sized you up very quickly. The moment he was satisfied, he relaxed. I asked him to tell me about the Moslem way of slaughtering an ox which is called *halaal* and he was very happy to explain the procedure, going through all the motions with his long knife and huge hands as if an invisible ox was there on the floor.

You tied its front legs and it back legs. Then about three other men held it down. Its head was forced sideways exposing the throat and then he described with great relish how the Imam drove in the knife and with one swift stroke severed the jugular. Death was just about instantaneous. "His eyes go pale, just like that," he said, snapping his fingers. The animal had to be killed by an Imam and it had to be left to bleed.

Looking out of the window of his shop towards the onion dome of a near-by mosque, you could feel Islam. Outside in the small lanes and narrow streets was the smell of curry and the fragrance and incense. Many of the streets, paved with stones, rise steeply up the slopes of Lion's Head. The quaint little houses are huddled together and rise each side in terraces forming rainbows of colour.

It is a different world, certainly the most eloquent part of Cape Town where the many different styles of houses seem to tell many fascinating stories. Many houses are beautifully restored, others are dilapidated. There is too much that is falling into ruin. The whole quarter, one feels, is finely balanced on that agonizing point between renewal and neglect.

Suddenly there is a face at a window, a beautiful Moslem woman, strangely Arabic, an embroidered pink veil falling softly about her oval face with its pale translucent skin. All the faces one sees are interesting, the same faces one sees in any Moslem city, some more Oriental than Arabic, some more of the Cape than of the East, varying from dark to the colour of brown paper and generally more controlled and sanguine than the faces one would see in, say, District Six. There are people everywhere: men in fezzes, men in overalls, men in perfectly tailored suits and small boys dressed like replicas of their fathers. They are purposeful people, lively and hard-working, their faith is sure, it's their courage and the mainspring of their lives.

One can spend some rich moments meandering through these lanes and streets, suddenly coming across delightful views of brightly coloured houses in rows beneath the serene Oriental ambience of a mosque with its silver star and crescent moon above a dome in the sky. As you walk higher, the views all round you become more spectacular. Look down from the top of Longmarket Street. It seems to hang like a broad belt between Lion's Head and the slopes of Devil's Peak, as if suspended, making a deep loop through the centre of Cape Town. From here the view of the Mountain is unrivalled.

You continue up Longmarket Street past Stadzicht Street, and Frederick Street. It is a steep climb over the cobble-like stones. An old man I met, grey-bearded and bent forward like a hoop, grunted up, placing one foot painfully in front of the other and stopping every five yards for a rest. "This kills you," he said. "It kills motor-cars too. No car lasts for more than a year up here. The roads are too steep."

Higher up you arrive at August Street. Turn right and walk to where it ends in a cul-de-sac and, laid out before you, is the greatest, widest and most spectacular view in South Africa. The whole of the city is spread at your feet. The view starts at Blaauwberg on the extreme left; it includes the whole of Table Bay and the Tygerberg, the entire Hottentots Holland almost as far as Gordon's Bay and Devil's Peak, Table Mountain and Lion's Head. It all forms a continuous panorama through an arc of about 280 degrees.

You can retrace your steps back along August Street towards the pink rows of flats in Schotsche Kloof. August Street turns into Voetboog Road which eventually runs into Upper Bloem Street and leads to a series of terraced steps into Bloem Street proper. At the corner of Bloem and Bryant streets is a delightful cluster of cottages in which the Moslem love of ornamentation frolics along the parapets. They are called the Arabian Cottages. Indeed with small shops selling mustard seed, cloves, cinnamon, and spices like methie, badia, jiera, koljanna and masala, the oriental influence is as heavy as a sweet scent.

When you decide to knock at a front door, the reception is always courteous. In one house there was a large silk embroidery with the words I have seen before in some mosques:

> Enthusiasm is the vehicle of my life
> Contemplation of Allah is my compassion
> Faith is the source of my power
> Sorrow is my friend
> Knowledge is my weapon
> Truth is my salvation
> Worship is my habit
> Love of all men is the core of my belief

No. 71 Wale Street where the Malay Quarter more or less begins, is quite a famous old house. For years it was dilapidated, but now it has been restored to its former glory. Conservationists and lovers of eighteenth century architecture in the Cape must look upon it with pride. It has a flat roof and a parapet with a wavy decorative moulding, and it was probably built between 1763 and 1768.

This house actually has a twin about fifty metres behind it which to me is a far more interesting building, firstly because it is owned and lived in, and secondly because, although it faces Buitengracht Street, it is half hidden behind another building and it is reached by a narrow lane. It has the same wavy parapet as 71 Wale Street and the interior is probably as genuine as you will find anywhere, with stinkwood beams supporting the roof and low interior doors of beautiful yellowwood. The owner, Mr Tohar Samson, is a proud man and very much aware of his obligation to keep this bit of Cape history alive. He believes, and I am inclined to agree with him, that his house was built a few years before the one at 71 Wale Street.

A walk along Jordaan Street towards Kloof Nek is rewarding. It is a narrow thoroughfare flanked on either side by the most fascinating jumble of dwellings, and it ends where the Malay Quarter ends at Whitford Street. Here is a sign which reads: "Up and down animal drawn traffic prohibited". A reminder of days now gone when the horse-drawn coaches, feathered and polished, were still used frequently by the Malays for their weddings and other celebrations. I haven't seen one for years.

The Malay Quarter is the only place left in South Africa where we can still get some idea and some feeling of what a street in Cape Town was like in the eighteenth century. This makes it a precious inheritance. And the Malays themselves are one of our most interesting communities. They always have been. Lady Duff Gordon's letters from the Cape in 1861 are filled with delightful descriptions of the Malays in those days. She knew them better than anyone else. She went into their homes, ate with them, drank their many beverages and treated their customs and religion with love and respect. They loved and respected her. Before she left the Cape, she wrote: "I shall grieve to think that I shall never see my Malay friends again. They are the only people here who are really interesting. I think they must be like the Turks in manners as they have all the Eastern gentlemanly ease and politeness; no Eastern obsequiousness and no idea of baksheesh; withall, frugal and industrious."

Far too little is known about the Moslem faith which is the most democratic in the world and one of the purest. In its essence it is pure theism, its cardinal principle being a belief in the power, unity, love and mercy of God. And it imposes rules of conduct without which no religion can influence ordinary fallible human beings.

Moslems believe that the universe, from the simplest form of life to constellations, is proof of God's existence and that God is one and indivisible, all-powerful, all-knowing, all-just, the Creator of heaven and earth, of life and death.

At the same time it is a reasonable faith. As long as the central doctrine of the unity of God and the message of the Prophet is acknowledged and accepted, it allows the widest latitude to human conscience. Everything human beings owe to one another, springs from this belief. The belief in God's grace and mercy is the very essence of the

Islamic creed. Their religion is a way of life and it is lived every day through its devotions. But the ritual of the Koran is simplicity itself. The essentials are purity of heart and self-denial.

Personal cleanliness was always an essential part of Moslem worship, it is a natural concomitant to moral purity. No man should approach God in state of uncleanliness, for an unclean body implies an unclean mind. The hands, the feet and the face should be washed before prayers are said except where conditions exist that make frequent ablutions impossible.

One of the great things about the faith is that, strictly speaking, there is no real priesthood. No other human being acts as an intermediary between God and man and this is where Islam differs from other creeds. Every man is his own priest. No sacrifice, no elaborate ceremony invented by vested interests, no ballyhoo is needed to bring the devout person nearer to God. This is what makes it such a democratic faith. It recognizes no distinction of race or colour. It repudiates all barriers of caste and class and it is this that explains the powerful fascination it has for people all over the world.

There is a belief in future life and accountability for human actions, in another existence. Man is not an accidental creation, and death on earth does not mean the end of the human soul, for the soul is an attribute of God and God exists forever.

One of the great strengths of the Moslem faith is its harmony with scientific thought. A theologian has put it this way: "Their religious doctrine of ceaseless accountability is identical with the scientific doctrine of ceaseless cause and effect. As science postulates matter and force are indestructible, so Islam postulates that the human soul is indestructible."

This belief in accountability has had some interesting effects in Moslem society. It has inspired Moslems with a sense of dignity and responsibility which makes suicide practically unheard of. Suicide used to be common among pagan Arabs as it is now among Christians. Moslems will fight to the death if necessary, but they will never take their own lives which they regard as a trust from God. To escape personal unhappiness or even unbearable pain through suicide, is considered an act of cowardice.

Fasting is prescribed as one of the lessons in self-denial, but inebriation is considered sinful. The dignity of labour, industry and thrift are all recognized, envy is condemned in the strongest terms, filial devotion is one of the highest duties and charity is one of the highest virtues, an act of purification. Pride and vanity are sins.

Moslems do not believe in hawking their faith or forcing it on others in any manner whatsoever, for belief can only come from God. There is no proselytizing.

Polygamy was lawful among most people of antiquity and it survived into the Moslem religion, but in most Moslem societies today it survives only in theory because the devout Moslem is allowed more than one wife only if he can deal with all of them with equity. If he can't do that he can only marry one. This rule has made polygamy virtually impossible for most people.

Kalk Bay

THE THREAT of removal under the Group Areas Act still hangs over one of the most deeply-rooted communities in the Peninsula – the Kalk Bay fishermen. Like all our Coloured people they are more characteristic of Cape Town and of the wind and the sea than any other group of human beings. One can only wish very devoutly that they will be allowed to stay where they are. Their relationship with the sea is a truly symbiotic one. Its salt, its smell, its many moods are part of their flesh and blood and their consciousness. It has shaped their lives and given them a culture of their own, a way of living and speaking, of thinking and dreaming. These things mean so much to people that nothing can ever replace them. They are the things that give life meaning. No-one and no authority has the moral right to take them away.

The Kalk Bay fishermen themselves seem to sense this. Their belief in their right to stay is so strong that their removal, if and when it comes, will be all the more brutal. One is aware of a marvellous cohesive force among them. Nothing will ever persuade them that their removal will be for the general good, that everything will be for the best in the long run. They are too tough-minded, too honest with themselves and with everyone else. The toughness of their lives has not only entered their bodies, it has given them spirit. They are a rough, hard breed accustomed to looking at life and death in the face.

I remember talking to a stocky old man who knew that he did not have long to live, a few weeks perhaps, a couple of months at the most. But he would not lie down and die, he still insisted on going out to sea as long as he had the strength. He was broad and bandy. He had strong stubby fingers and his fingernails had grown thick from work. He was a cancer sufferer and had lost his voice. Surgeons had removed his vocal chords. He wore an open-neck shirt and there was a hole at the base of his throat just above the breast-bone. If you looked into the hole you could see the inside of his chest. It was through this hole that he breathed. He also used it for smoking. He loved rolling his own cigarettes which he did with one hand.

He would put the cigarette in his mouth, roll it along his lips, light up and inhale deeply. Then he would blow the smoke out through the hole in his chest and take a great delight in watching the reaction of people all round him. I dare say it was a kind of party trick. It was frightening until you got used to it. He could even blow smoke rings through the hole and would take wagers all round that he could blow better smoke rings than anyone else. There was something indestructible about the spirit of this man. He would not lie down and die, he would not give in and you felt that he would never really crack inside. You felt that he would go on fishing as long as he could and that even on his death-bed, he would blow smoke rings with his very last breath.

Yes, the Kalk Bay fishermen are a rough, hard breed. There is no doubt in their minds what their rights are; there is no place for double talk in their rough productive lives. As a community they are tightly bound together by toil and tradition, by faith and integrity and – by the sea. They spring from varied stock: Portuguese, Phillipino, Javanese, English, Irish, Afrikaans and Cape Coloured.

They are both Christians and Moslem. But you can safely say that all of them are the offspring of the wind and the sea. They are and always have been, seamen and fishermen. Few people in South Africa have a deeper sense of belonging to the mountain and sea environment that is theirs. Even those families who years ago were forced to go and live "up the line" still regard Kalk Bay as home. They come all the way from Heathfield and Steenberg to worship in their Kalk Bay church on Sundays. Their fathers helped to build the St James Catholic Church.

Few people appear to be more positively conscious of what is theirs, not by law, but by usage, by love and devotion and that intuitive knowledge of the sea and ships handed down to them over a dozen generations. Theirs is certainly the right to use this knowledge. But they cannot use it unless they live by the sea.

They do not own Kalk Bay and only a few of them own their own houses. But Kalk Bay is theirs in the sense that they have largely made it what it is. They have given it its atmosphere and character. Without them it will be something quite different. They have also inherited the right that comes from making themselves useful to their fellow men. "We feed thousands of people," one of them said with a smile that showed the longest row of gold teeth in the Peninsula.

In a way these indefinable rights add up to something that is morally unassailable. It gives them every reason to stay where they are. They are convinced of this and so are most of the Whites who live in Kalk

Bay. However, being realists, they are more concerned about the practical impossibilities of taking fishermen away from the sea when the sea is the whole reason for their existence. They never stop thinking or talking about the sea. When they are not out in their boats they are constantly watching it because there are many things that tell them what the chances are of a good catch: the direction of the wind, the colour or "look" of the water, the temperature, the currents, the movement of the birds.

As one of the veterans said: "How can you watch these things if you are living on the Cape Flats? It is vital for us to keep an eye on the many changes of weather that suddenly come over False Bay. We all know how suddenly the weather in the Peninsula can change and only the fisherman knows how this affects the fish. I have fished the whole coast from South West Africa to Port Elizabeth, but conditions at False Bay are quite different. Even our boats are different: they have a wider beam and deeper draught, and our fishermen are probably the best line men in the world and I'll tell you why.

"The Irish and English stock from which many of them come, all came off the old sailing ships, they were thoroughly trained and disciplined seamen who passed their knowledge down to us. And they blended with the Javanese and Phillipinos who were the best fishermen in the world. This unique combination produced the Kalk Bay fishermen."

He explained how important it was for them to live at the sea and know its play with the wind. Geelbek will not bite with a south-east or southerly wind, but they will bite with all the westerly winds. As a rule snoek refuse to bite with a south-east or east wind, but they will bite with all west winds. Yellow-tail will bite with all northerly winds, but not with southerly winds. Knowing the temperatures is important because few fish will bite when the water is very cold, and temperatures are affected by the wind. The movement of the sea birds is another sign fishermen always look for; birds follow the shoals of small fish and the small fish are followed by the big fish.

Often there are patches of coloured water that move with the currents. Experienced fishermen can tell from the colour of the water what the temperature is and at what depth the fish are likely to be. Different parts of False Bay can have a dozen different temperatures at the same time, and all this affects the movements and the behaviour of the fish.

Fishing from Kalk Bay then is already a difficult and complicated business. If the fishermen were forced to live elsewhere it would become impossible and many of them would lose a livelihood because they have no heart to do anything else. Any skipper will tell you that if conditions suddenly become favourable, he can assemble his crew in five minutes. They are all there living together, within whistling distance. But if the community was scattered over the Peninsula it would be impossible to get them together and down to the boats before conditions changed, perhaps for the worse.

Then there is the fear all of them have that if they were moved from the sea, their traditional knowledge and skills would die within a generation and one of the greatest sea traditions of the Cape would die with them. Another old veteran said: "We can only gain and pass on our knowledge to our children by living at the sea. I went down to the harbour with my father when I was three and from that day on I was a Kalk Bay fisherman. It is the same with my own son. If we ever have to leave here our children will be attracted to other trades. Everything we know that is of value will vanish."

But their removal from Kalk Bay would mean so much more than that. It wouldn't just be a removal, it would be cutting at the roots of what is part of history. The ancestors of the Kalk Bay fishermen took root there nearly 200 years ago. Many of them were survivors of wrecked Portuguese merchantmen. The old romantic names are still there in the baptismal and marriage registers of the St James Church: De la Cruz, Bonaventura, Eustachio, Da Silva, Gomez, Quimpo, Herminigildo, Ortega, Marcranus, Aquilar, Oriego, Fernandez, Almacin, Lipari, Andrade and others.

The old marriage registers going back to the middle of the last century show how they gradually intermarried with Coloured people, English and Afrikaners. A Gomez married a Miss de Vos, a Da los Santos married a Miss Smit, a De Sa married a Miss Howe, a Damaso married a Miss Haylett.

Later on towards the end of the century, men with English names started marrying the dusky daughters of the fishermen. A Mr Searle married Josephine Gomez, a Mr Jurgens married Anna Quimpo, a fellow called Burns took the vows with Louisa Carvalho.

Not many of these names are left today. How completely the process of integration took place can perhaps be gauged by glancing at the school register of the St James Mission School attended almost entirely by the children of the Kalk Bay fishermen: Cronje, Essau, Lee, Pepino, Davis, Gomez, Trimm, Woodward, Basson, Coetzee, De la Cruz, Redelinghuys, Erispa, Geldenhuys, Gordon, O'Shea, Wessels, McCauley.

In fact what has emerged is a society completely different in outlook, way of life and often in appearance from the other Coloured people of the Cape. They are a self-contained pocket with their own traditions, school, church, mosque, cinema, shops and homes, even their own way of speaking. At the same time they have evolved as part of the whole Kalk Bay community. The trust and respect between them and the Whites is something quite special.

Crime is practically unknown among them. A police station established at Kalk Bay "to keep an eye on them" closed down years ago because there was nothing to do. It is one place in the Peninsula where there has never been any hooliganism. The Whites have made the fishermen feel that they have a stake in Kalk Bay, not only because they own many boats costing a lot of money, but because they are a deeply-rooted stable community with their own carefully guarded standards and values.

Here, Whites and Coloureds have built up their own communal spirit. There is no encroachment by the one group on the sensibilities of the other. They have achieved a unique situation in which there is both perfect integration and segregation, because it is voluntary and not forced. It is one of those examples in South Africa that leads one to think that if apartheid suddenly disappeared from the scene, life would go on in very much the same way, except that it would be far more interesting.

Vanishing Pubs

ONE OF the charms of Cape Town not so long ago were the number of small pubs in the central city area and the incredible variety of human types they managed to produce. Well, they didn't produce them, they merely attracted them and, having attracted them, brought out and magnified their various hidden qualities.

The results were that at certain hours of the day there were a lot of free-swinging characters in this town who enlivened the local scene and made a considerable contribution to the friendliness and the human quality of the city. There were scores of pubs at street level and on every working day of the week they were full. They obviously supplied a social need. To hundreds of characters they were a second home, to some they were the only home. They were the ordinary man's club. In them he could relax and be his uninhibited self.

He could even be larger than himself. The strangest of associations grew up in pubs, little drinking associations, schools and fraternities and they were always the centre of intense and lively discussion on just about every topic under the sun.

Everyone had his own favourite pub and certain types drank in certain pubs. Printers always used to drink in the Thatched Tavern in Greenmarket Square, artisans frequented the Johannesburg, the Harp and the Mountain View in Long Street. For some reason or other the old Standard used to attract most of the queers. Journalists, writers and artists stuck to the Café Royal, advertising men preferred the Green Hansom, the Metropole and the Manchester. Generally every one of them was a happy port of call and they were so distributed round the centre of Cape Town that this city provided one of the most spectacular pub crawls in the world.

All that has gone, most of the characters have gone. The Gresham, the Brooklyn, the Trocadera, the Cumberland, the Imperial, the Stanley, the White House, the Del Monico. They read like a roll of honour. They have all gone and scores of others with them.

The Government forced dozens of them to close with its sweeping classification laws. At one stage thirty establishments closed down in eighteen months. It simply didn't pay a bar or hotel owner to stay in business when he had to spend thousands of rands to keep on the right side of the law. The city has never been the same since.

Fortunately the most famous of them all is still there in Church Street although it has changed considerably – the Café Royal. It is truly the most famous pub in South Africa and I am happy to have been associated with it for nearly thirty years. It has been the meeting, drinking and arguing place of writers, artists, lawyers, architects, printers, publishers, politicians and journalists since the turn of the century. It is dark, uncomfortable, unattractive, cold in winter, hot in summer and even sordid looking at times, but the only customers it ever lost were those who owed money or died. Its restaurant which adjoins the pub has fed some world-famous figures and gourmets.

From the gourmet's point of view, it has had good years and bad years, but its atmosphere has remained unique. Its decor with red satin and mirrors, is the same as it was at the turn of the century. The bar has been the club of one of the most extraordinary drinking fraternities South Africa has ever seen and in the constant sieving process some gems of human types have been uncovered and their performances at various times have indeed ranged from the sublime to the ridiculous.

Many of them are dead, some are nearly dead, others should have been dead long ago, large numbers of them are still alive, even if they are not fully aware of the fact. I dare say that pub types are duplicated all over the world, but the Café Royal types are the only ones I have ever known. Of the hundreds of *habitués*, I don't think that more than ten of them were alcoholics or died-in-the-wool drunks. Most of them were social drinkers who found the companionship and the company of the Café Royal irresistible.

There was a time when it must have been one of the wittiest, bawdiest, most blasphemous, most intelligent, happiest and most entertaining pubs in the world.

The counter in the Café Royal bar was always known as The Mahogany. It was so named by one of the establishment's hardest drinking *habitués* who not so many years ago left this life to join what he hoped would be another spirit world. Somehow the name stuck and it is still used by today's front-liners or first team drinkers as a kind of memorial to a brave and big-hearted imbiber. Men who frequent bars go about the ritual in more or less the same way wherever they are. They will go to their favourite pub every day at the same time of the day and most regulars stand at exactly the same spot in the pub. If they have to move only a few inches one way or the other they feel uncomfortable and often aggrieved. There are always those who will enter and leave a pub two or three times before settling down to the serious business of the day. There are shy drinkers, stylish drinkers, nervous drinkers who develop facial twitches as soon as they raise a glass, and drinkers who approach their alcohol with reverence. There are silent drinkers and guilty drinkers whose eyes often roll round the rim of the glass, pompous drinkers, masochistic drinkers who swallow the stuff with an anguished shudder, and the uncomplicated, down-to-earth men who just get on with it.

Every pub has its class and pecking order. A stranger or newcomer has little chance of making the grade unless there is general approval. Similar types gravitate towards one another and this gregarianism has produced that fascinating social phenomenon called the "drinking school".

There are normally a number of schools in every pub, each school with its own part of the pub, its own drinking habits, its own brand of conversation and humour and its own way of paying for the drinks. Some schools go "Dutch", meaning that every man pays for himself; in others each member of the school is obliged to buy a round and anyone who doesn't is not regarded as one of the boys; he faces ostracism. And every pub has its elder statesmen, usually customers with long and loyal service who unconsciously set the tone.

As a forum of discussion, the Café Royal in its best days was unequalled. The place was always full of newspapermen, critics, artists, lawyers and various other professionals who were expert in their fields. Discussion was always very intense and serious, often passionate and heated, but there was always a ring of truth about it. It was here that you would find the most honest assessment of a new play, an art exhibition, a ballet or opera, a new novel, a murder trial or any event of social or political importance.

Alcohol was not the only stimulant. Ideas kept arguments going till late in the evening. And if you wanted to keep abreast of Cape Town gossip, the Café Royal was the focal point of it all. It always was, and still is, the favourite pub of many artists and newspapermen and, because both professions seem to attract so many eccentrics, the Café Royal became the stage of a number of memorable characters.

The restaurant was once renowned for its food. Lawrence Green said that at one stage it was as good as any restaurant in Europe. Yehudi Menuhin thought the food was superb. Irma Stern, who was a gourmet, was always an angry patron, but a patron nevertheless. So was Judge Andrew Beyers. When he was Prime Minister, Mr J. G. Strijdom often dined there. The American gourmet, Maurice Dreicer went there in his everlasting search for the perfect steak which has taken him to nearly every country in the world. He didn't find it in the Café Royal, but he loved the place.

Dreicer was a gourmet's gourmet. He carried a silver butter knife with him wherever he went and said that when he could cut his steak with it, that would be the perfect steak. He also had with him his steak thermometer and a solid ball of gold on a chain which he used for testing the consistency of caviar. His sole concern in life was nourishment. He lived for food.

Dreicer said that compared with the highest culinary standards, cooking in Cape Town restaurants varied between not-good-enough and average. Cooking, however, had deteriorated all over the world and one of the main reasons was the disappearance of the old coal stove. All really great restaurants used coal stoves or charcoal. South African crayfish was the best in the world and our wines were excellent.

Asked what his choice would be if he knew that he could have only one more meal on this earth, Dreicer said:

"I'd start off with caviar that has passed my gold ball test and I'd have a little vodka with it. Then a good turtle soup with some dry Spanish sherry. After this a fine steak, preferably United States prime. It must be perfectly grilled, black on the outside, pink inside and red in the centre. With the steak, a French salad and some grilled tomatoes. And, most important, a bottle of Chateau Margaux, a French burgandy that costs R36 a time. This I'd follow up with a little Strasbourg *foie gras* with vintage port. For dessert, a champagne sherbert with a nice cognac and a Havana cigar. After that I don't mind if they carry me out with my toes up."

The Café Royal did, in fact, have a coal stove in the days when Mr. Strijdom, who was then Prime Minister, used to dine there. The coal lorry arrived late one night when Mr. Strijdom was having a private dinner party in the restaurant. In those days the restaurant and bar

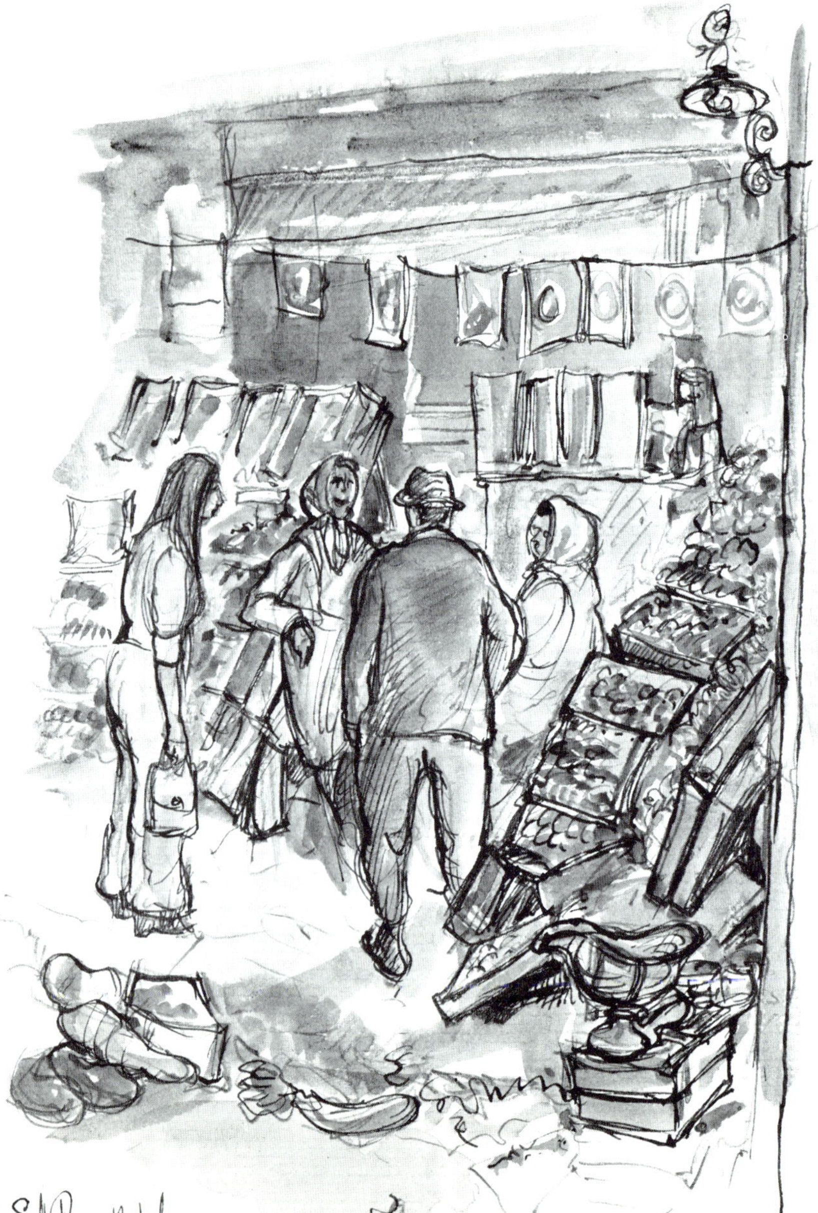

Salt River Market.

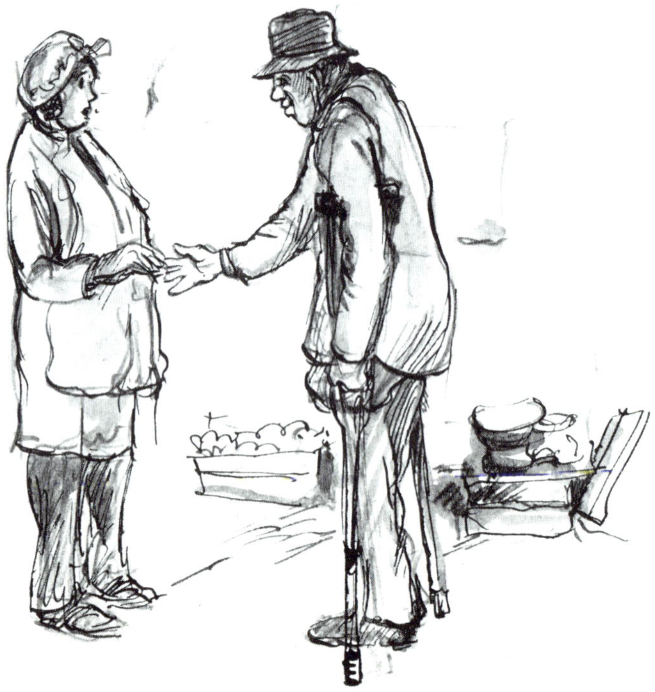

Arms

were joined by an interleading swing door. It happened to be a pay day and Jock Webster, a rumbustious *Cape Times* Press photographer was going wild in the bar. Suddenly four Africans carrying huge sacks of coal on their backs appeared in the bar. The Africans, covered in coal dust, looked very black indeed. They also looked rather bewildered. They wanted to dump their loads of coal, but didn't know the way to the back yard. Jock Webster who was by now thoroughly inebriated, shouted: "Follow me!" Instead of showing them through the door to the yard, he showed them through the door to the restaurant. And into the restaurant they marched as the Prime Minister and his guests were busy with their dessert.

One of the most aristocratic and enigmatic Café Royal *habitués* was a man called Champagne Charlie. He was tall and superior and never said a word to anyone. No-one knew who he was or where he came from, but he made his appearance at 6.30 every Friday evening, always dressed immaculately in a dark suit, a grey Homberg and a red carnation in his buttonhole. He always entered through the west-side swing door and walked straight to the back of the pub where a chair and small table were set aside for him. He would hang his Homberg on a peg and sit down facing the wall, his back to the crowd, seemingly oblivious of everyone else.

He was always served by a barman called Vic who would spread a clean white napkin over the table and place on it a silver ice bucket and a champagne glass. The bottle had to be opened in Champagne Charlie's presence and it was always Pieper Heidsick. Champagne Charlie would contemplate the bottle in the ice bucket for a full five minutes before donning a pair of grey gloves which he always used for drinking. Then he would pour the first glass with tremendous care and reverence and sip it very slowly, as if he was toasting a ghost or trying to communicate with someone who wasn't there. He used to stay for exactly an hour, finishing the bottle on the stroke of 7.30 when a chauffeur driven Rolls-Bentley would pull up outside and hoot the letter R in the morse code.

This would be the signal for Champagne Charlie to remove his gloves, fold them, put them in his inside breast pocket, stand up, smell the red carnation in his buttonhole and walk out as silently as he had walked in.

The ritual went on for many months. Every Friday Vic would have the ice bucket and the glass waiting for Champagne Charlie's arrival at 6.30. Then one Friday Champagne Charlie never turned up. He was never seen in the Café Royal again and as far as I know he was never again heard of. Not even Vic knew what had happened to him. "All I can tell you," Vic said, "was that he never tipped me less than a pound."

It was a lot of money in those days. Champagne Charlie did things in style.

The New City

THERE doesn't seem to be much that we ordinary people can do about saving what is left of old Cape Town or about shaping the city's future. Everything seems to be out of our hands; it is the experts who have all the say. All we can do is lodge protests which nearly always come too late and, as far as I'm aware, have never had the slightest influence on the decision makers. We, the ordinary people, tend to be over-emotional about everything and, even worse, we know little and understand even less. But we know at least one thing because we are seeing it happening. We know that in Cape Town the quality of our human environment is gradually deteriorating.

There are many reasons for this, some of them we are not even aware of, but I would say the three most obvious are the ascendancy of the motor-car, the multifarious laws and by-laws that are regulating every aspect of our lives: moral, social, economic, intellectual and spiritual, and the negative impact on the environment of buildings that have grown beyond every human scale. But it is nobody's fault; it has just happened, slowly and accumulatively. It has been done piecemeal without anyone foreseeing or understanding the consequences.

The result is that instead of restricting the traffic flow into the city, everything has been done to make it easier for more cars to come in. So now we have four giant parking blocks and more such buildings to come for an ever-increasing number of vehicles which stand idle for most of the day. The provision for parking alone has become a major industry in South Africa involving hundreds of millions of rands a year. These garages, however, haven't taken the parking load off the streets and squares which are more congested than ever. Every street is like a concrete bowl, spiked with an excrescence of parking meters, robots and traffic signs.

Exhaust pollution, the noise, the annoyance, the frustration and the tempers of motorist and pedestrian alike are things we have come to live with. In fact, motor-cars have taken over the city from the human being. It is not something that is happening. It has already happened and it is going to be extremely difficult to reverse the process.

As for the heavy mesh of laws and regulations, there seems to be little doubt that South Africans are living in one of the most regimented societies in the world. The individual, no matter what his race, is being restricted economically, socially and in the manner in which he might like to earn his living or conduct his personal life. This has made everyone less effective and less motivated than he should be. It has made everyone less of a full human being and we are rapidly becoming a nation of compliant lap dogs, held by our rulers on invisible leashes. All these statutory laws have affected Cape Town more than other cities because, traditionally, there was so much more here to break down and unscramble. There is no doubt at all that these laws have had a deep effect on moods and attitudes and the general feeling of harmony that was once so evident in the city.

This is an aspect of change that is so subtle that it is not always noticeable. The salve of goodwill that still remains has taken the hurt out of many wounds. But there is nothing subtle about the revolution in the physical shape of the city. It is advertised in towering blocks of steel, glass and concrete, all shouting to high heaven. They have entirely changed the profile of Cape Town, changed the streets and the once easygoing atmosphere. They have even increased the velocity of the wind as anyone knows who has walked round these skyscrapers when the south-easter blows. It's because these buildings are often so stark, arrogant and intrusive that they have angered the layman. But in my opinion this anger is misplaced.

Modern architecture is one of the things that arouses the critical faculties of the layman to a violent pitch. So do modern painting, sculpture and music. They seem to threaten him with a world he doesn't yet understand and is not yet prepared to accept, although he will in time. The layman's aesthetic approach to the arts is traditional and the gap between that approach and the advances made in the arts is almost unbridgeable. So all communication breaks down.

I can understand the general disillusionment with modern painting which very often has not been intellectually honest in the sense that some artists have put their work on an abstract philosophical plane which everyone knows is beyond the painter's own mental capacity. It is this that gives the layman the feeling that he is being taken for a ride.

But I don't see how he can have the same feeling about modern architecture, no matter how unpleasant he finds it, because the intentions of the architect are honest. He hasn't the same freedom of aesthetic expression as he used to have or as the painter or sculptor has.

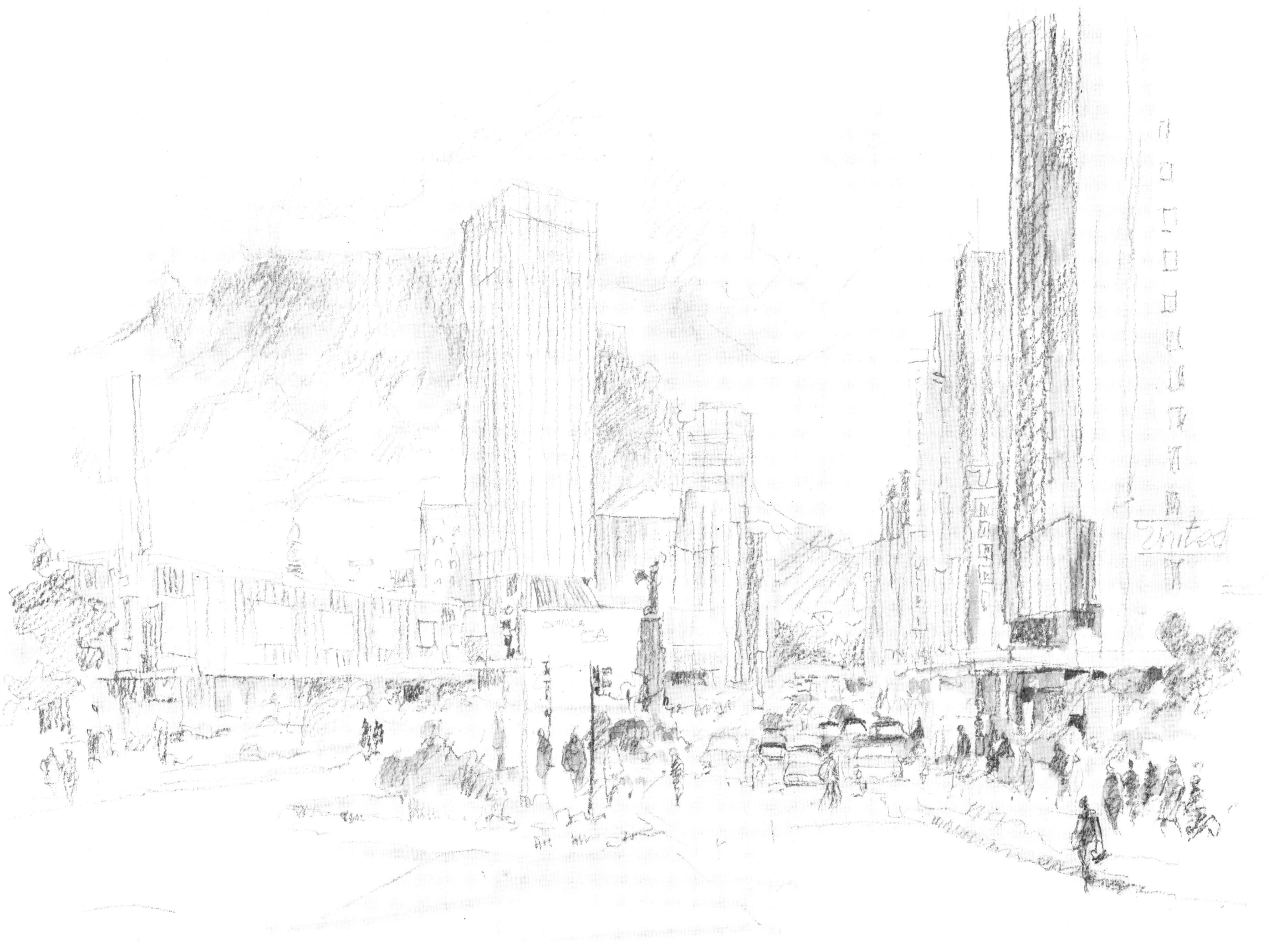
United

There is in fact a fundamental difference between painting and sculpture on the one hand and architecture on the other: whereas the content of painting and sculpture is essentially aesthetic and evocative, architecture today is merely functional and supplements the science of modern construction. Architecture is there to serve a purpose and a function and not to stir the emotions.

Modern architecture cannot be solely judged as an art, for it depends primarily on the application of scientific principles and must meet the demands of climate, social need, modern methods of construction and modern materials available. Above all it must be appropriate to its times.

I personally don't think there is anything wrong with modern architecture as such. It is a logical development from the past and it could not have developed in any other way. While some buildings are ugly, others are thrilling and even breathtaking. But there is one thing about some of them, which is unacceptable and that is the far-reaching effects they are having on our street environment and therefore on the human quality of our city. We still get that life and contact in some of our streets, notably Long Street, Plein Street, Church Street, Loop Street, Bree Street, Longmarket and Shortmarket streets, Hout Street and others. They all still have a special character, atmosphere and warmth. Walking along them we are in touch with many minds and ideas, many smells and interesting enclaves. But walking past a modern concrete block we are in touch with only one vision. All the life that once filled a street is now being pushed upwards into a huge perpendicular capsule beyond our physical and emotional reach and encased in a veritable tombstone.

Too many of these buildings seem to be repeating some of the worst features of the old monumental style of public building, where dead areas are being created at street level. This is where they seem to be dehumanizing life in the city. When one walks past them, there are no rows of shops but one continuous blank wall.

There are many examples, public buildings mostly, and they are creating dead areas all over Cape Town. They are all part of a growing uniformity, of a tendency to encase everyone in a kind of artificial, sterile, air-conditioned, necropolis in which people do nothing but arrive, work and go home.

T. S. Eliot once wrote that a culture may be described simply as that which makes life worth living. Will the new city taking shape before our eyes give us such a culture? One sincerely hopes that it will.